Going Rackless

Going Rackless

Chicago's Amateur Pool Players and the Quest for Glory in the Biggest Tournament in the World

DYLAN TAYLOR-LEHMAN

3 FIELDS BOOKS
An imprint of the University of Illinois Press

3 Fields Books is an imprint of the University of Illinois Press.

© 2025 by the Board of Trustees
of the University of Illinois
All rights reserved
Manufactured in the United States of America
P 5 4 3 2 1
♾ This book is printed on acid-free paper.

Cataloging data available from the Library of Congress
LCCN 2025013232
ISBN 978-0-252-08889-6 (paper : alk.)
ISBN 978-0-252-04833-3 (ebook)

To the entire ZMA crew,
My team past, present, and future

The billiard world has also found a Mecca in Chicago. Some of the greatest experts in the world first came to the surface in this city. The perfection in the manufacture of implements of the game has been achieved here, and the greatest tournaments find their field within Chicago's walls. Thus it is that this city has reached a very pinnacle, indeed, in the world of sports, such as no city ever held in this country before and which no other city is ever liable to win. . . . In all other matters of sport she has a place near the top, and is always looked upon as a prime factor in any gathering of sportsmen.

—*Chicago's First Half Century*, 1883

I am not a very good billiards player, and I do not doubt that I wrote this history of the game to placate my sense of inadequacy.

—Kenneth Cohen, "Billiards and American Culture"

Contents

A Note on Methodology

Work on this project began when I began visiting City Pool Hall and playing on a team not long after I moved to Chicago in the fall of 2019. I played once a week and made visits to that hall (and others) when I wasn't playing, and at the same time I began researching the history of the game in Chicago and of pool more broadly. The COVID pandemic put league play on hold, and after moving away from Chicago for approximately a year, I returned in the middle of 2021 and jumped back into the project with renewed vigor. While I no longer was on a team, I made regular visits to pool halls to watch the teams I was following, take in miscellaneous matches, and conduct interviews with the people profiled in the book (and many who weren't). Further interviews took place in peoples' homes and businesses, including interviews with scholars, business owners, and historians of various aspects of Chicagoana. I attended the 2021 and 2022 World Pool Championships in Las Vegas, where I continued to follow the teams at the center of the book and interviewed dozens more people attending and working the events. I took in countless games over the course of this project, the written accounts of some of which were helped by online videos of the matches, and I followed up with many interviewees to clarify events, quotations, history, and motivations. My interviews with players and others are quoted without citation throughout the book.

League Operators and Team Rosters

League Operators

Chicago Central APA: Ross Schaefer
Chicago APA: Brad Hall
Chicago Central APA and Chicago APA Assistant: Gregg Taylor

Team Rosters at the 2020–2021 World Pool Championships and the 2022 Chicago APA Citywides

WAKE AND BREAK

2020–2021
Jutichai "Jedi" Vatanagul (Captain)
Sonia "Blade" Aujla
Damo "Blackout" Moloney
Matt Rink
Oscar Sandoval
Jorge Mora
Jesus Perez
Owen Tracy Bacucang

2022
Jutichai "Jedi" Vatanagul (Captain)
Sonia "Blade" Aujla
Damo "Blackout" Moloney
Matt Rink
Oscar Sandoval
Jorge Mora
Spicy Tobiason
Isaac Sommerville

KICKIN' LIKE BRUCE

2020–2021
Vincent "Bo" Lee (Captain)
Brian Hale
Cynthia Tang
Lyn Panabi-Dumagpi
Jennifer Mui
Victor Mui
Wayne "Bubba" Mui
Wayne Wong

2022
Vincent "Bo" Lee (Captain)
Brian Hale
Cynthia Tang
Lyn Panabi-Dumagpi
Jennifer Mui
Victor Mui
Wayne "Bubba" Mui
Wayne Wong

BB CUES

2020–2021
Adina Fried (Captain)
Alison Lewis
Vivian Ramos
Christine Degrange
Teresa Jimmerson

2022
Adina Fried (Captain)
Alison Lewis
Taylor Peterson
Trisha Kimber
Jeannie Zhu

BILLIARD MEN

2020–2021
Eli Mancha (Captain)
Christine Arce
Pierre Kasiansky
Ryan Morse
Ricky Torres
Jackson May
Ricardo Cagnetta
Jon Ruiz

2022
Eli Mancha (Captain)
Christine Arce
Pierre Kasiansky
Ryan Morse
Ducky Borteli
Janet Momero
Mike Desnoyers
Jan Novotny

One Day at Citywides

Jutichai "Jay" Vatanagul was doing his customary dance around the pool table one muggy June evening at a pool hall just west of downtown Chicago. He held his cue out over the table to assess the angle of a potential shot before darting to the opposite side to consider another. A t-shirt and expensive gym shorts facilitated his loose style of play, and he discreetly hit a vape pen here and there to calm his nerves.

In addition to accommodating the quirks of the table and the pressure of being watched by dozens of his peers, Vatanagul also had to contend with how the dank summer weather impacted the game: Hands get stickier, wooden cues expand, and the green felt on the table becomes saturated by heavy air, which affects the way balls glide. Players adjust how they play to account for these minute differences, but this in turn can compromise some of the finesse and control needed to win.

One way to counteract the weather was the vaguely threatening, slightly sexual-seeming black glove Vatanagul was wearing, a piece of nylon that covered his first two fingers, thumb, and part of his palm. The glove is worn to reduce friction between fingers and cue, and so far it had made a noticeable difference in how he played. It was an enhancement he'd adopted a few months earlier, and he unconsciously tugged at the hem as he continued to analyze the table. Weather aside, he was already being much more deliberate than usual, as this was no ordinary game.

Vatanagul was the captain of a team called Wake and Break, and the team was competing in what might be the deciding match of the American Poolplayers Association's 2021 Chicago citywide tournament. Two rounds of tournament play had reduced an entire league's worth of teams down to just Wake and Break and their opponent, and Vatanagul's teammates sat in the shadows just beyond the table, legs and cues bouncing as they watched the increasingly tense match.

Vatanagul sank a few balls and then missed, giving his opponent the chance to whittle the number of balls down significantly. The 8 ball was left sitting by itself along a rail, and Vatanagul looked over apologetically at his team for allowing things to get to this point. But then the crowd gasped: His opponent hit the ball more softly than he should have, and it petered to a stop before hitting either ball or rail. That was a scratch, which meant ball in hand—Vatanagul could lay down the cue ball and shoot from wherever he wanted.

"I analyze a lot of situations to make the optimal choice," he later said, drawing a parallel between pool and his job as a cybersecurity specialist. "I'm confident in what I can do. But the trick is being consistent." Fortunately, he had been shooting consistently all day, but still, he felt the pressure in the room even more acutely as he allowed himself to think about what was at stake.

Should Vatanagul make his shot, Wake and Break would prove the team not only the best in the league but possibly in the entire country: The winner of the citywide tournament would get an all-expenses-paid trip to Las Vegas to compete in the World Pool Championships, the Superbowl of nonprofessional league play and the biggest pool tournament in the world. Should Vatanagul choke, as his opponent inexplicably just had, then the hopes and dreams of the entire previous season, stretched to more than eighteen months on account of the COVID pandemic, would be for naught.

After another tug at his glove, he set the cue ball in position.

Hosted each year by the American Poolplayers Association, the World Pool Championships bring more than thirteen thousand players to the Westgate Resort and Casino for almost two straight weeks of pool. The world championships are the final showdown between citywide champions from all over the country who duke it out across acres of pool tables in a massive single-elimination tournament. The biggest events are the 8-Ball and 9-Ball tournaments, with around one thousand teams each, but there are also the Women's, Doubles, Captains, and Wheelchair championships (among many others) and smaller-scale buy-in tournaments running 24/7 alongside the major events.

When players aren't competing, which they sometimes do for more than twelve hours per day, they're attending clinics, taking in product demos, watching trickshot artists, ordering custom cues, and browsing dozens of booths selling every accessory known to the sport. In Las Vegas, everything is an "experience"—there's the Italian Supercar Driving Experience and a risqué revue called "Men: The Experience"—and the World Pool Championships absolutely qualify as Pool: The Experience.

The APA consists only of amateur players, and one of the league's main draws is that each team must have a balance of abilities in order to compete. That means beginners play alongside seasoned old heads, providing players of all skill levels with an encouraging but competitive way to play pool. The average league night will see bankers, builders, bartenders, lawyers, stylists, salesmen, and florists shooting it out together, the majority of whom are gunning to make it to citywides and beyond.

Each year, there are three APA seasons that send players to citywides, and the World Pool Championships are the carrot at the end of the stick that validates the substantial amount of time, money, and effort each player and team puts into the sport. Championship matches are played in front of hundreds of spectators and are live-streamed at "almost ESPN quality," as APA national marketing director Jason Bowman says, with commentators, professional lighting, and numerous cameras, including an overhead shot of the table replete with diagrams and analysis. "We want to take amateur players and put them on a pedestal. We look at it very much like a production, a show, an experience. We do it on a scale much larger and much greater than most."

Wake and Break, like many other teams, considers making it to citywides the minimum standard for a successful season, a chance to prove to your pool-obsessed peers that it is your team that's the best. This shared ambition brings teammates together as a family-like unit, a bond that only deepens after playing together for years on end.

Vatanagul is one of Wake and Break's three co-founders alongside Sonia "Blade" Aujla, who works in the insurance industry, and Damo "Blackout" Moloney, an Irishman who has worked as a chef in Chicago for almost twenty years. Aujla and Vatanagul used to work together, and it was she who introduced him to the APA in 2017. They met for a drink to shoot and catch up and, noticing their tabletop chemistry, Vatanagul was easily talked into joining the team Aujla was putting together. "Sonia was always the coolest one at work," Vatanagul said. "We were impressed she was going to a Las Vegas pool tournament—the rest of us just went home at night!"

A little while later, they saw Moloney shooting at a different bar, staying on the table as he burned through successive challengers. "We need this guy," Aujla said, nodding at the slaughter. Moloney admitted he was a bit drunk when he agreed to join the team and realized the next morning that he forgot to tell them someone had recently stolen his cues from his car. *Too bad*, he shrugged, *now I have a reason to get new equipment.* That was four years and countless games ago, and now the trio finish each other's sentences and say, "No, you tell it!" when recounting a team story.

The three count on each other to take their commitment seriously, and they've adapted other aspects of their lives to accommodate pool. Aujla and Vatanagul are single, having no time for or interest in a relationship, and Moloney, who is married, knows that the late nights spent playing pool are not necessarily conducive to marital bliss. "Normally we have a rule—no couples," Vatanagul said. "They're either going to break up or they fight, and you have to choose a side."

Wake and Break had qualified for citywides in late 2019, but the Coronavirus pandemic meant that the event wouldn't be held until almost a year and a half later, in the summer of 2021. Vatanagul managed to get in some table time at bars that left their back doors open for trusted patrons, but the team hadn't played together in more than a year by the time vaccines were rolled out and the race to Vegas was back on. Consequently, a few teammates had been walloped early on at citywides, but things steadily turned around as the team got back into their rhythm. When Vatanagul's opponent failed to sink the 8 ball on an open table, Wake and Break were given a gift to bring the match home.

Vatanagul got into position. His chin, stick, and feet formed a straight line that ended a few inches from a precise spot on the cue ball.

Citywides was on the line.

Vegas was on the line.

It was go time.

His stick pumped forward with the elegance of a nurse giving an injection. The cue ball glided across the table and connected with the waiting 8, which shot forward and landed with a clunk in the corner pocket. The cue ball curved away and came to a stop in the middle of the table, as safe as can be.

A perfect shot.

The noise of the room swelled back to normal as if Vatanagul's ears had taken a breath of fresh air, and he heard the telltale rattle of the ball through the table's insides.

"That game was nail-biting, hair-raising, nerve-wracking, a little bit of everything," Vatanagul later said. "We each had three heart attacks."

Heart attack or no, Wake and Break had just secured a trip to the World Pool Championships. Based on how he felt at that moment, he had a good feeling about how the team would do in Vegas. But Wake and Break were not alone in their regional glory and ambitions. The team would be joined by other Chicago teams who'd earned similar passage, all just as confident that *they* were the real ambassadors of Chicago pool, ready to harness the city's history of hustlers and grimy dives to prove it.

As any serious pool shooter knows, if there is a meaning to life, the highs and lows of a good game come as close as anything to revealing it. The search for that meaning would feel especially intense on the tables of the World Pool Championships, now only a few months away.

PART I

Welcome to the Chicago APA

CHAPTER 1

A School for the Game
Learning the Ropes at City Pool Hall

City Pool Hall, where Wake and Break clinched their trip to Vegas, is one of the major hubs of American Poolplayers Association league play in Chicago and an ideal place to start for those interested in taking the game more seriously.

Tucked away near some train tracks at 640 West Hubbard just west of the Loop, Chicago's skyscraper-filled business district, City Pool Hall is a squat, single-story building that glows like a cozy tavern in the winter and has umbrellas and motorcycles out front in the summer. Smokers stand outside ripping heaters no matter the weather, grunting hello to the players walking in with quiver-like pool bags slung over their shoulders. Once their cigarettes are finished, the smokers likewise head in to the table they'd been assigned for the night.

Players are greeted by a rush of warm air as they push past City Pool Hall's glass doors and are enveloped by the sound of clacking balls and overlapping conversations and televised Chicago sports. To the right is a little-used dining area with a handful of booths and to the left is the three-thousand–square-foot room with nine pool tables laid out in a grid. More than one hundred players fill the hall on a busy league night, with a 65:35 ratio of men to women and players ranging in age from their thirties to their sixties. A number of people will be eating dinner before the first game starts, either bar food classics or something from the establishment's surprisingly good home-cooked specials, which are written on chalkboards throughout the hall.

City Pool Hall opened in 1999 with the intention of catering to league play, which now happens almost every night of the week. Most patrons play 8-Ball, the classic game of solids and stripes, but there is also a steady contingent for

9-Ball, a punchier game in which both players try to sink balls 1 through 9 in numerical order. The focus is almost totally on pool, from players trading tips to such paintings as *Game of Fate*, in which Marilyn Monroe and the Three Stooges watch James Dean and Humphrey Bogart shoot around. At one point, a couple took their engagement photos at the exact table where they'd met during a match. "He was really drunk and said I had a nice ass," the bride-to-be said. "I told him to fuck off. But the next week he came over and apologized and wanted to make it up to me. And now we're here!"

I made my way to City Pool Hall for the first time one puddly, noir-like evening in the fall of 2019, the air crisp and smelling unexpectedly of chocolate thanks to the smog pumped out by a candy factory nearby. I'd recently started living in Chicago and, having always enjoyed pool, figured that playing the game would be an interesting way to get to know the imposing city. After doing a little bit of research, I found out there were some local leagues that fought to play in a massive tournament in Las Vegas, and Ross Schaefer, the operator of the Chicago Central APA league, was quick to offer me a spot on a team to get an even closer look at the world of league pool. I was assigned to a Thursday night 8-ball team and would be starting in the middle of the sixteen-week fall session. I was told to ask for a man named Chalkie, the captain of my team, once I arrived.

I saw that most people were drinking, and drinks seem to materialize in people's hands thanks to roaming servers who know not only everyone's name but beverage of choice and numerous details from their personal lives. "I don't know how I do it. It just comes to me. I'm just meant to do this, as sad as it is," laughed a server named Miranda, who splits her working hours between City Pool Hall and an upscale country music bar. A back patio with large glass windows allows players to keep an eye on the games as they smoke. In particularly tense matches, players will duck out between turns, leaving a still-burning cigarette on the windowsill for the next time it's their opponent's turn to shoot.

I followed the winding bar to a back corner near the patio door, not sure of the politest way to navigate around so many people shooting at once. The bar ended at a waist-high glass display case full of City Pool Hall merchandise and various pool accessories from hats to gloves to the iCue, a ball with a target-like graphic on it designed to help players learn different shots. The counter is where civilians reserve tables when they're not occupied by league play and where APA players pick up a manila envelope containing the evening's score sheets, which contain the names and rankings of players on both teams and have a complex but logical way of keeping track of the action of each game.

Taped to the countertop is an overhead sketch of the room's table layout. Each table, labeled from 1 through 9, has the evening's matchup written on it, and I saw this meant matchups between such teams as Shoot to Thrill and Ruth Bader Winsburg, the Chi Racks and the Chi Town Shooters, or The Midnight Strokers and The Island of Lost Souls. Every league boasts more than a few teams whose names are puns on "balls" or "shafts," but Renee Glenn, who's managed City Pool Hall for almost as long as it has been open and greets almost every player by name as they come to the table, barely notices anymore. I asked her to please point me in the direction of my captain and she gestured at a table on the paper on the counter.

Chalkie's Children? I thought. *That's the name of my team?*

The team's name was an homage to captain Ron "Chalkie" Aguirre, who, like the other captains, sat at a high table alongside the pool table and analyzed the evening's matchup. He said he was glad to have me because the team had recently lost a player and needed someone to pick up the slack, in both competition and paying weekly dues. That evening we'd be playing the Midnight Strokers, a team Chalkie said was "all right."

Chalkie makes his living managing the apartment building he owns after a long stint as a graphic designer, seemingly specializing in the rock 'n' roll aesthetic, judging by the stocking cap pulled low and the tribal design on his shirt. He was typically quite calm when he was playing, but he had the moving, thinking eyes of a pool player, and random twitches of his arm or leg gave away feelings his face would not.

Each APA team has eight players, and five of them must be present to play each week. Regular season play generally lasts twelve to fourteen weeks, with each season having a final tournament that in turn qualifies teams for citywides. Regular season play consists of up to five separate matches of multiple games each, the exact number of which is determined by the players' handicaps, as lower-ranked players need to win proportionally fewer games to take a match. A team needs ten total points to win the night, with two points awarded for a victory, one point for getting "on the hill" (losing the match but winning a certain number of games), and three points for a "shut out," in which you don't let your opponent win a single game. In APA 8-Ball, skill levels run from 2 to 7, with 7 being the best, and in 9-Ball, from 1 to 9. While there are no restrictions on who can play whom, team captains generally try to put players against opponents of equal skill. Smaller leagues often see teams playing each other a few times per season, and part of the strategy involves knowing players' strengths and weaknesses. But in larger leagues teams might only play each other once per season, the unfamiliarity with how each team plays making for a challenge of its own.

8-Ball Games Must Win Chart

Your Opponent

Skill Level	2	3	4	5	6	7
2	2/2	2/3	2/4	2/5	2/6	2/7
3	3/2	2/2	2/3	2/4	2/5	2/6
4	4/2	3/2	3/3	3/4	3/5	2/5
5	5/2	4/2	4/3	4/4	4/5	3/5
6	6/2	5/2	5/3	5/4	5/5	4/5
7	7/2	6/2	5/2	5/3	5/4	5/5

(You — left axis)

9-Ball Points Required To Win Chart

Player's Skill Level	Points Must Win
1	14
2	19
3	25
4	31
5	38
6	46
7	55
8	65
9	75

"The Equalizer," the APA's handicapping system, enables players of different abilities to compete more fairly against each other by adjusting the number of games a player needs to win in order to take a match. (Courtesy of poolplayers.com.)

Team captains not only coach their teams but also make sure players show up each night to shoot. Depending on the handicap algorithm, a single match could consist of as many as eight games, which means the average evening of APA pool can easily last until midnight or beyond. After a long day of work, less-committed players want to be the first to play so they can go home early, as players are not obligated to be present the entire time their team is playing. When few people are enthusiastic about staying late, this can cause problems with team cohesion and morale, especially when the vibe is off across the many weeks of regular season play. But players serious about making it to the World Pool Championships tend not to care about how long they'll be shooting. As Eli Mancha, captain of a team favored to go to Vegas called The Billiard Men, explained, he expects his teammates to show up on time and try as hard as they can each and every night. "There are some people who just want a night away from their wives and just want to drink," he said. "Those players aren't on my team."

Chalkie's Children did not share this competitive approach. I would quickly learn that the team was more like a way station for players entering the league and a repository for players whose teams disbanded. The rotating cast of characters meant that a shared sense of purpose, and thus the team's prospects for going to Vegas, weren't particularly high. But I was warmly welcomed onto the team and made my rounds shaking hands and learning names.

At the time, my fellow Children included Neil (skill level 5), who was dressed in all black with a Fraggle-like head of thick black hair who worked in bioinformatics, "poking around the genes of viruses and bacteria"; Harnish (6), a wiry dude known to line up and take his shots perhaps too quickly; Rachel (3), who'd been playing bar pool for ten years and wanted to take her game up a notch; Kevin (7), an exceptionally good if somewhat frazzled player who was only semi-reliable in terms of attendance; Valentin (3), a boisterous, fun-loving middle-aged guy retired from the metal brackets business, and James Terronez (4), who, with his sweater vest, shaved head, and clenching jaw, looked like a football coach. I paid attention to the rhythm of being on a team and listened closely to pool banter, trying to get a sense of what *topspin* and *pocket speed* meant. "If I could shoot pool with my mind and not my hands, I'd never lose," Kevin said. *Very true*, I thought.

The concentration of players around tables became much denser as 7 p.m. drew near, and everyone was piecing together equipment and pulling on gloves. A few minutes later, the floor around each table cleared as the first players from each team got ready to shoot. Players "lag" to see who goes first, shooting a ball down the long side of the table so it bounces back, with the player who gets it to stop closest to the rail breaking first. The mood in the hall grew noticeably more serious as people got in the zone. Etiquette dictates that nobody stands close to the tables or in the shooter's line of sight when a game is in session, and the servers patiently held trays aloft as they waited tableside so as to not break someone's concentration. Teammates also generally avoid talking to whoever is playing, as active players get one coach per game and don't want to waste it on idle conversation.

I would be third in the evening's lineup, which could either be fairly soon or in a few hours depending on how fast everyone shot. As I waited, Chalkie explained the basics of the game's strategy. Pool is not just about sinking balls but about "position play," or shooting in such a way that you not only make your shot but leave the cue ball positioned for the next. That's why good players can win in one turn: They look for the best route around the table and are capable of pulling off the interconnected series of shots that make it happen.

At that point, I'd been shooting more frequently than I probably ever had in my life thanks to the table in the mezzanine of the office building where I worked at the time. That table was on the verge of falling apart, and the end of the single usable stick had a plastic ferrule (tip holder) that was so compressed and cracked I expected it to break apart with every shot. Nevertheless, I was able to string together some good runs and figured that the ability to overcome these deficiencies meant that I would fare even better with proper equipment. *It sure would be a great narrative turn if my team made it to Vegas while I'm writing this book*, I thought, secretly envisioning myself as being the one to set this triumph in motion. But most of my competitive experience had been no-stakes games with friends at home or in a bar, and my playing had certainly never been scrutinized by a dozen players on two teams. When Chalkie laid out the basics of pool's real strategy and technique, I realized the game was much deeper than I'd expected and that everyone in the room was already much better and more confident in their games.

And while I did own a pool cue that I got at Kmart years earlier, for some reason I didn't think to bring it that first evening and was thus further disadvantaged by not having a familiar piece of equipment. Players who take the game even semi-seriously will have their own cue, and the countless pool bags propped up against chairs or hanging from hooks along the wall suggested that everyone in the room was quite dedicated to the game.

Most pool bags are leather or leatherette cylinders about 2.5 feet tall and five inches in diameter and typically contain a shooting cue and a breaking cue, which unscrew in the middle and rest snugly in padded slots. The breaking cue is used exclusively for breaking (so as to not compress the tip of the shooting cue), and some players carry an extra shaft or two on top of this for good measure. In the bag's various side pockets are pool gloves, chalk cubes, bridge heads, tip shapers, tip scuffers, shaft smoothers, and other tools for making minute adjustments to the stick. Some players carry an APA rulebook, a notebook, and a roll of quarters, and many bags have plastic luggage tags that attest to the player's willingness to travel for a good game. Many bags have keyrings on the outside that collect the APA patches that players have earned. There's a patch for a "Break and Run," in which every ball is sunk in succession with no missed shots, for "Going Rackless," or winning all of your games and thus not having to rack, and the "I Beat the League Operator" patch, which hints at the paternal, somewhat cranky relationship between operators and players.

Some high-level players have invested in cues that cost hundreds or even thousands of dollars, but many players, like my fellow Chalkie's Child James Terronez, prefer equipment with deep personal significance. He used a Meucci-brand, Larry Hubbart[1] edition butt, which was given to him by his dad more than forty years ago and for which he commissioned a specialty shaft. The comfort of a trusted piece is priceless, and in the evening's first game against the Midnight Strokers, Terronez bent over and shot in a practiced, fluid motion, sinking one ball right after the other. He was wearing headphones and his head bobbed to music only he could hear.

"What's he listening to, Tony Robbins?" said one observer. "He must be hearing, '*win, win, win, win*.'"

---

1. Hubbart, incidentally, is one of the founders of the APA.

Terronez finally missed, but he didn't leave his opponent with a good shot. Players can employ a defensive maneuver called a "safety," in which the cue ball is shot not at an object ball with the intention of sinking it but to leave it inconveniently positioned for the opponent. With no ball to make, Terronez's opponent executed a safety that sent the cue ball to rest lightly between a ball and a rail.

From the outside, safeties may not seem impressive or daring, and at one point, they were considered unmanly and could legitimately provoke a fight. "Back in the day, no matter what the position, you took your shot [at a ball]," said Freddie Norris, who runs a pool hall called Twisted Rose in Algonquin, a northwestern Chicago suburb. "I still feel guilty about doing safeties." In some places it still might raise an eyebrow if you play too conservatively, but playing defensively is simply playing smart, the strategy and skill set an integral part of the game.

The safety didn't stop Terronez, however, and he quickly reduced the remaining balls down to the 8, with the cue ball only a few feet from its target. He didn't even need to take the final shot; his opponent pushed the 8 ball into the nearby pocket to acknowledge that he lost and was eager to get the next game started. The table was quickly re-racked, and the crack of the break resounded through the air.

Soon enough, it was my turn to play.

My debut match was against Reggie "The Riddler" Julun, a 3 who my teammates said was decent but not consistent. Tall and tattooed, Julun was wearing a hat that said "Riddle This" and didn't say much as we got ready to play.

"The game isn't about those balls, it's about this one here," Chalkie said, pointing to the cue ball. "Make sure you know that." OK, I nodded, gripping my cue.

My first game was middling, and I tried to resist the impulse every player has to explain, "I don't usually miss shots like that." I lost but felt great in the second game, going on a rally and sinking the 8 ball for the win by bouncing it off a rail into a far corner pocket. This was 85 percent by accident, but the bystanders' modest praise bumped my confidence up significantly. My swagger was promptly demolished in the next game when I just couldn't seem to make even the most basic shot. I tried slowing down and taking my time, tried speeding up and following my impulses, and tried hitting harder and softer, but the balls just would not behave how I wanted them to. Chalkie said encouraging things but remained expressionless, and once or twice I thought I saw him wince but try to hide it.

The Riddler finally took the match after the next game, and walking away from the table, I thought of the first time I went to a driving range. *How hard could golf be?* I laughed to myself before somehow hitting backward into the shelter so it ricocheted crazily from wall to wall, like in a cartoon. I apologized the next day to a guy I knew on the golf team for making fun of the sport, and I similarly apologized to Chalkie's Children for my performance, feeling like I'd oversold myself.

"Don't worry," said Kevin, a 7 and outright incredible player. "I've played something like 1,200 APA matches. And I'm still not that good."

Shit, I thought. *If he thought he was bad, I was even worse than I thought.*

I told Neil I was interested in following a team to the Vegas championships for a book I wanted to write. He looked skeptically at the score sheet.

"Well, I think you're on the wrong team if you want to do that."

"Hey!" James Terronez said. But his umbrage waned and he dozed off, having commuted almost two hours early that morning from the suburbs to his job in the city.

A few hours and many games later, teammates at City Pool Hall and other APA-affiliated venues across Chicago started closing out tabs and packing up gear as tired-looking players got ready to shoot their final matches. I was glad to step out of the spotlight when my match was over but also wished I could keep playing all night. As a certain intergalactic hermit-sage once said, I'd taken my first step into a larger world, and although I'd been at the hall for hours by this point, I was very much looking forward to coming back the following week.

As the fall session went on, I soaked up as much about the game as I could and paid careful attention to how my teammates played. Though it must have been excruciating for skilled players to watch newbies push balls around the table as we missed easy shots, it was exciting to see my incremental gains in ability play out on the table and feel my understanding of pool physics grow. Ross Schaefer said people were drawn to league play because it provided a thrill and a challenge they'd been missing in their lives, and he was right about the energizing impact of that competition. At one point I was peeling an apple and found myself imagining I was competing for the longest and thinnest continuous peel. I would've won, of course, judging by the two unbroken feet of curly skin I'd produced, and if the thrill of an imaginary crowd cheering me on for peeling fruit was invigorating, imagine what pulling off a game-winning shot must feel like!

The Chicago Central APA's fall session went on until mid-December and then reconvened in early January 2020 to finish its final matches. Chalkie evidently had gotten married in the interim, and Miranda the server was proud to show off how she'd upgraded the tattoo on her right temple. The three stars that had been there before were joined by at least twelve more. "Someone told me it looked like I didn't have any face tattoos," she said. "So I had to prove I did!" Unfortunately, but somewhat expectedly, Chalkie's Children didn't make it to citywides; we didn't even make it to our league's qualifying tournament.

The spring 2020 session began after a short break, and I continued playing with Chalkie's Children, which had swapped out two players for two guys who happened to be tenants in the building Chalkie owned. We played some decent games, but once again, our record was not promising. It was a moot point anyway. News of a strange virus started making the rounds, and pool—along with much of the rest of the world—was soon put on hold. When league play resumed almost exactly a year later, I left my playing days behind me and instead focused on following the efforts of some more promising teams attempting to make it to Las Vegas, surely a more exciting topic than chronicling my own attempts to go from terrible to slightly less bad.

CHAPTER 2

Portrait of a League Operator
The Man Who Facilitates the Madness

As league operator, Ross Schaefer is in charge of the Chicago Central APA, the man who facilitates the madness for hundreds of players seven days a week. Tall, bespectacled, with slightly unkempt shoulder-length hair and clad in jeans and a casual sport jacket, Schaefer performs weekly duties including registering players, dropping off score sheets, collecting dues, tabulating statistics, and promoting the league and its various tournaments. He's also responsible for doling out the funds for the annual trips to Las Vegas, which, in the Chicago Central APA, means money for the flights and lodging for the approximately fifty people who earned passage, as individuals or as part of a team.

"Sometimes people can be confused when I explain my job to them," Schaefer said with a shrug and a grin. "It was a hobby that became a profession."

Though Schaefer doesn't typically attend many regular-season games, he is on call every night there is league play and often must field calls about rules when he's working on a non-pool project or out on a date.[1] As the highest local authority to whom players can appeal, he's made a conscious effort over the years to distance himself from the league's social drama and hopes that this precludes accusations of playing favorites. Schaefer does attend all major tournaments, given the higher stakes and likelihood of dispute, and he was on hand for the 2021 citywide tournament (in which Wake and Break won their trip to Vegas), overseeing things with former APA league owner and grizzled pool vet Gregg Taylor. The pair observed the proceedings from their de facto command center, two small tables that had been pushed together in

---

1. "Think of it this way—1,500 people have my phone number, and most of them aren't calling to tell me I'm doing a good job," as one league operator from St. Louis put it.

the dining area and piled high with pens, score sheets, laptops, phones, and a portable printer and strewn with used napkins, plates, and cups.

A swimmer and tennis player in high school, Schaefer picked up darts and pool in college and started playing in the Chicago Central APA in 2006 under league operator Brad Hall and then under Taylor when Taylor bought the league. Schaefer said he was a captain who was always getting in Taylor's ear about how to improve the league or new bars he might consider expanding into. As it happened, Taylor was looking for a successor, and, appreciating Schaefer's passion and smarts, approached him about buying the league in 2012. Schaefer was taken aback by the offer, but having been a player himself, he understood the appeal of the league. Not only did it provide a much-needed social outlet, but he knew the prospect of a trip to the World Pool Championships was the perfect incentive: It's attainable, democratic, and overall a pretty nice reward for playing pool. He had won a trip four times in six years himself, and one of the reasons he considered *not* buying the league was that he didn't want to give up being a player.

At the time, Schaefer was thirty years old and going through that bout of self-reflection that comes when you suddenly realize you're supposed to be an established adult. The more he thought about it, the more being a league operator seemed like an interesting gig, almost certainly less oppressive than whatever more traditional job he might find himself doing. He decided to go for it, and, after passing a criminal background check and an in-person vibe check with the APA, he used his life savings, some money from his parents, and a substantial contractual loan from Taylor to take over the Chicago Central APA league.

Schaefer then went through the weeklong training at the APA headquarters in St. Louis that all new operators must take to familiarize themselves with the rigors and standards of running a league. Though it rarely happens, the APA has the power to come in and take over a franchise if the owner can't follow the guidelines, sometimes even forcing the owner to sell, but Schaefer has had a successful career as an operator. Sometimes he works ten hours a week, sometimes more than seventy, but it's a self-propelling system that generates consistent income thanks to the schedule of year-round play.

Generally, the value of a league is determined by multiplying the number of active teams by $3,000, and the leagues in Chicago easily have more than one hundred teams each. Some leagues are busy enough that they hire assistants or pay people to handle administrative duties and help run tournaments, which was the case with Gregg Taylor, who's retired from the operating business but still active in the scene. Being an APA operator also requires a lot of marketing and social media activity to promote the league and continually bring in new players, which Schaefer admits isn't a task he enjoys.

The COVID-19 pandemic greatly affected everything about league play. Because it was an eating and drinking establishment, City Pool Hall had to close in March 2020, about a third of the way through the spring APA session. Although many establishments found technical ways around the rules to stay open, Ross Schaefer erred on the side of caution when it came to his league and opted to shutter play. It wasn't a popular choice, he said, but he went with what the majority of the players wanted.

There was certainly a newfound sense of excitement in the air once regular pool play began again and the 2021 citywide tournament was able to take place. As at every citywides, there were a few complaints about a questionable shot or issues with someone's tabletop behavior, but perhaps because people were simply happy to be playing again after the pandemic, there were no allegations of note. All of the teams that continued to win and progress through the tournament were considered to have done so fair and square, and all the teams that got knocked out of the tournament took their losses gracefully.

Still, the stakes at citywides are quite high, and it is in circumstances like these that one might be most inclined to attempt to game the system. It is a risky move, to be sure—cheating can get offenders banned from the APA for two years—but it is nevertheless something that league operators must contend with from time to time. Though it's not in Schaefer's natural disposition to act like a school principal, navigating the allegations of impropriety that occasionally arise is one of the many responsibilities he has grown to handle since he started running the league. Ironically, it is the handicapping system designed to make the game as accessible as possible that is at the center of most of these disputes. A brief digression will explain why this is the case.

In the late 1970s, Terry "Texas Terry" Bell and Larry "The Iceman" Hubbart were part of a group of pool players who met with investors interested in starting a professional pool tour. Both were experienced shooters who made a living traveling around the country and playing pool, but after sitting in on the meeting, Bell felt that developing a new professional circuit wasn't the best way to grow the sport or make more money for players. Instead, he suggested, the group should focus on bringing in as many new players as they could, thereby growing a fanbase that would support a professional league further down the road. "They looked at me like I was a stone idiot," he recalled, but Hubbart thought this was a good idea, and the two decided to start a team-based league that would welcome players of all abilities.

The pair agreed that Bell would run the organization from St. Louis, Missouri, while Hubbart—nicknamed The Iceman because "you'd get cold waiting for him to miss"—would hit the road again as a player to fund their work. Neither was the partying type (a rarity for the roadbound pool cowboy); they preferred instead to work on the league over a nice dinner once the playing was over for the day. The league had its first big break in 1979 when it paired up with sponsor Anheuser-Busch, the beer giant also located in St. Louis and an obvious choice given that most pool tables were in bars.

Bell and Hubbart hustled to grow what was called the Busch Pool League and navigate the financial precarity this meant for their families, who rented apartments next to each other in order to carpool more efficiently. The league's first World Pool Championships were held in St. Louis in 1981 across twelve tables and with a combined prize purse of $12,000. The league continued to expand from there despite constant name changes, going from the Busch Pool League to the American Pool League to the Bud Light Pool League to the Camel Pool League when RJ Reynolds Tobacco got "extremely involved" as a sponsor. A wave of lawsuits in the late nineties eventually led to prohibitions on tobacco companies' sponsoring sporting events,[2] but by then the league was self-sustaining, with 175,000 members, and eventually rebranded itself the American Poolplayers Association. The APA is still privately owned by the Bell and Hubbart families today and boasts around sixty employees at its headquarters in a St. Louis suburb called Lake Saint Louis, where they oversee the league's more than three hundred franchises and organize the massive tournaments and miscellaneous branded events held each year.[3]

While an overarching NFL- or MLB-style pro league has not emerged as the go-to league for pool (more about why not later), Bell and Hubbart certainly succeeded in their goal of bringing more people to the game. Today, the APA is by far the largest amateur or professional pool organization in the United States, with a quarter million members playing in every state, as well as in Canada and Japan.[4] The APA's largest single league is in Boston, which has more than a thousand teams, and Florida is the state with the greatest number of players overall. The largest concentration of APA players in the United States is in and around Chicago, ranging from the three dense leagues in the city proper to the numerous leagues throughout the Chicagoland suburbs.

---

2. The RJ Reynolds company also started pool's Camel Pro Tour, which then disappeared as well.

3. The APA World Pool Championships have a sister tournament called the APA Poolplayer Championships, which host the championship events for individuals and doubles teams. They also include the 8-Ball Classic and 9-Ball Shootout, the 8-Ball and 9-Ball Doubles Championships, the Jack & Jill and Masters Championships, and the Team Captains and Wheelchair Championships. This event is also held at the Westgate, is typically held in May, and is as grandiose as the fall tournament but slightly smaller.

4. There, the leagues are known as the Canadian Poolplayers Association and the Japanese Poolplayers Association.

While the APA is the nation's biggest pool league, it is by no means the only one, and each league has its own expected level of ability. The same hall will often host a few different leagues, with a section of wall dedicated to displaying plaques, trophies, and team photos. On Mondays, for example, City Pool Hall hosts a small American Cue Sports league (another amateur league) alongside the APA 9-Ball teams.[5] But the APA's ubiquity and welcoming structure make it the preeminent league in the country, because few other leagues offer beginners a chance to play on a team from day one. The APA is "organized, competitive, and friendly," as Ross Schaefer put it, a good balance of players who want to play casually after work and players who place the Vegas-bound competition at the center of their ambitions. "It will help you get better at pool. It will help you go into bars and feel comfortable and ready to take someone on," he said.

The league's accessibility is facilitated by "The Equalizer," the APA's proprietary handicapping system. Players in the APA are rated from skill level 1 to skill level 7, with a player's handicap roughly corresponding to how many balls he or she should be able to sink in a row (which, in turn, speaks to that player's understanding of the game's theory and technique). A player's handicap determines how many games he or she needs to win per match, meaning that if a 3 took on a 5, the 3 would have to win two games and the 5 would have to win four games to take the match.

Players new to the APA automatically start at a 3, more or less reflecting the expected skill set of the average bar shooter, with their ranking rising or falling from there. Some people have a natural facility for the game, while others grind away on frustrating plateaus between noticeable improvements. Going from a 2 to a 3 to a 4 takes work but is attainable for the average player; jumping from a 5 to a 6 to a 7 is another story, though, because the increase in skill is almost exponential, and in many respects it becomes a different game altogether.

The cumulative handicap of the five teammates playing on a given night cannot exceed 23, which requires a balanced roster including lower-ranked players. This is why captains pay such close attention to who will be coming to play each night. They must field players strategically to mirror their opponents at each match. I once saw a team put a player at level 2 against a 6, the only possible matchup after everyone else had played. The 2 obviously got destroyed, an example of what can happen when players aren't serious about showing up.

---

5. The league is home to a few players who've been exiled from the APA, and the interaction between the two was like when you encounter an ex, polite enough but purposefully aloof.

The results of every single APA-sanctioned game affect a player's handicap almost in real time, whether a game in the regular season, a tournament, or a one-off APA event. This means that a player's ranking can change in the middle of citywides or the World Poolplayer Championships, throwing off the team's crucial handicap balance when it matters most.

This is where "sandbagging," perhaps the most controversial aspect of the APA, can come into play.

Sandbagging is when players will pretend to be worse than they are to gain a low handicap, which means they need to win fewer games than their opponent in order to take a match. Then, when it counts, for instance, at citywides, they play at their real ability level and easily take down the less-skilled opponents they're matched with.

Some say sandbagging happens only occasionally and that fluctuations in performance reflect the good and bad streaks that any player goes through. Or, players might not be playing up to their ability because they're trying out new techniques, especially if they've already qualified for Vegas in a previous session and can afford to take it easy. But according to one player who asked to remain anonymous given the controversial nature of the following assessment, sandbagging happens so frequently (and even so artfully) that it is essentially part of the APA style of play. At the extreme end of the spectrum, the player said, he's seen people play left-handed for an entire season but switch back to their dominant right hand for a tournament. But if the sandbagging is subtle enough, a player might be able to get away with it.

And that's what happened the following year at the 2022 citywides. A team called Sinking Every Complicated Shot (SECS) accused a few players on the Ramen Boys team of playing much better than their nominal on-paper ranking would indicate. Schaefer and Taylor were aware of the accusations and were monitoring the game from City Pool Hall's patio, their faces and hands pressed against the glass as in a cartoon.

One of the SECS shooters made a huge "You see?!" gesture at them when a 2 made a very difficult shot.

"No biggie, just a full-table thin cut shot," the opponent said, rolling his eyes. "I'm a 7 and I never make that shit."

Sandbagging is widely derided and decried for an obvious reason—it's cheating—and players can take their pick from a wide variety of anti-sandbagging merchandise at the Las Vegas championships, including the knockoff Calvin peeing on the word *sandbaggers*. The APA is not amused by the practice, either, no matter how elegantly it's done, and does whatever it can to catch it. League operators are required to send the winning teams' score sheets to the APA headquarters so that staff can go over every single game inning by inning[6] to make sure the stats make sense. If irregularities are found, the APA will correct players' handicaps to place them where they should be. A drastic increase in a short amount of time is likely indicative of sandbagging and thus prompts a deeper investigation, which, in turn, could lead to the two-year ban.

Based on a quick assessment of the 2022 citywide score sheets and the preceding season's worth of team stats, Taylor acknowledged in private that it did appear that Ramen Boys *were* sandbagging and that he was aware of the rumors that the team wasn't shy about employing such a tactic. It was a shame, he said, because there were some really promising players on the team who were either unknowingly associating with bad actors or were themselves getting sucked into doing something unethical.

"In the real world, these guys would be charged with fraud, manipulation. One lawyer with a briefcase can steal more than ten men with guns," Taylor said with a knowing look.

Soon enough, Schaefer found himself trailed by two equally pissed-off teams and was trying to hear their concerns as they followed him from one side of City Pool Hall to the other. Schaefer emphasized that his league and the APA are very friendly and ethical places to play overall, and not seeing enough evidence either way to take sides, he offered to get on the phone with the main APA office to get their take on how the problem should be solved. It was in the spirit of tabletop camaraderie that the Ramen Boys were ultimately given the benefit of the doubt: their victory at the citywides *would* count, and they would be allowed to keep moving forward in the tournament. A few players' handicaps would be raised because there was no way around the fact that they should be raised, and the team was, in effect, put on final warning: If anything even remotely suspicious took place, the Ramen Boys would be done. Both teams accepted the ruling without expression, accepting the outcome but not happy with it.

"Some call that shitty pool; here we call it 'Championship pool,'" one player muttered.

Schaefer shrugged, willing to be the bad guy if it meant making the game as fair as can be.

"I just want a fair match," he said. "Some say I play favorites, but it's important for me to stay neutral. Honestly, I'm the strictest with the people I know best."

---

6. In pool, an inning is a completed cycle in which both players have gone up to shoot. Games between good players will have only a few innings (or sometimes only one); on a score sheet, games between newer players look like the tallies of days marked off on a cave wall on a deserted island.

CHAPTER 3

Legacy of the Felt

9-Ball, Kickin' Like Bruce, and the History of Pool

> Recreation and amusement, so necessary to the
> symmetrical development of all our lives, are
> denied to those most needy of it—or rather, they
> are supplied in abundance, but of a character and
> under circumstances not conducive to good morals.
> —Royal L. Melendy, "The Saloon in Chicago, Il."

In March 1819, not long after the state was founded, the Illinois General Assembly passed in its first session "An Act for the Prevention of Vice and Immorality," which prohibited residents from playing "cards, dice, billiards, bowls, shovel board, or any game of hazard." The idea was to curtail behaviors inimical to the development of the state and to rein in the loss of large sums of money through gambling on these games. The fine for violating the act started at $10 per offense ($258 in 2025 dollars) and was raised over the years as the law expanded to prohibit the sale of equipment such as playing cards and pool tables.

Laws such as this did not make the idea of settling in Illinois particularly appealing. Its eventual repeal led to the opening of Chicagoland's first pool hall in 1831, six years before Chicago was chartered as a city. Guidebooks and business registries would go on to list dozens of pool halls within city limits by the end of the nineteenth century, not including the tables in saloons, barbershops, and various quasi-legal establishments, which likely pushed the number of tables into the hundreds or thousands.[1]

---

1. The podcast *99% Invisible* put the number at 831, or more than the combined number of gas stations, McDonalds, and Starbucks in Chicago today, whereas the 1901 study "The Saloon in Chicago, Il." quoted at the start of the chapter says that there were 143 pool halls in 1901.

The lineage of pool rooms eventually led to places such as City Pool Hall, which took over the building housing a gothic dance club called Gotham, which in turn was previously an auto garage and before that a small machine shop during World War II. The building has no columns that would obstruct shots, and City Pool Hall was the first in the country to use high-end Brunswick Gold Crown IV tables.

Krystal Glenn has worked at City Pool Hall since the early 2000s and currently manages the bar. Her parents owned a bar when she was growing up and were good friends with the couple who started the first APA leagues in Chicago in the 1980s. Her father, Glenn Glenn, at one point held the record for most APA matches played, at almost three thousand. She's been playing pool since she could "barely see over the table—and now I'm tall!" and knows a lot about the lives and dramas of the hall's patrons because many of them have been coming to play as long as she's worked there.

The feel of City Pool Hall is incredibly familiar, in some cases literally so. Krystal's mom is Renee Glenn, the manager who runs the pool counter, and her nephews are Christian, a bartender and server who's worked there since 2014, and Michael, a lanky bartender in his twenties with a curly mullet and leather vest who looks as if he stepped out of *Dazed and Confused*. The venue is located at the end of a street where it terminates in a bridge, making the place feel like a secret hideout. Glenn says she'll routinely have people stumble in and say they'd never heard of the place despite living nearby. "Our local firemen didn't know we existed. But once people come here, they love it here. It's like home. It's weird if you don't have a good time and never come back."

Just as playing there lends itself to an insular camaraderie, so, too, does playing 9-Ball, the second-most-popular billiards game in the United States and the second-largest event at the APA's World Pool Championships. Monday nights are 9-Ball nights at City Pool Hall, and the teams in this league take a small amount of pride in playing a game the casual shooter might not be familiar with. The game has its own lingo, strategy, taunts, and technique, and while the local 9-Ball division has fewer shooters than does the 8-Ball division, it certainly has no less spirit.

The game of 9-Ball tends to move quickly because it only uses balls 1 through 9, which are racked in the shape of a diamond and which both players attempt to sink in numerical order. Each ball you pocket is worth one point and the nine is worth two, with points continually tallied across multiple games until one of the players reaches a predetermined number of points. There are many players who enjoy both 8-Ball and 9-Ball—"I'm bi-pooler," as one t-shirt put it—but for those who get hooked by 9-Ball, it can be hard to come back from the punchy nature of the game.

"There's lots of thinking [in 8-Ball]—more thinking than I'm willing to do," laughed Vincent "Bo" Lee, co-captain of Kickin' Like Bruce, a Chicago Central APA 9-Ball team that qualified for the 2020–2021 World Pool Championships.

In Las Vegas, the end of the 8-Ball tournament overlaps with the start of 9-Ball. Kickin' Like Bruce won its slot in Vegas at the long-awaited post-COVID 9-Ball citywides in June 2021, though co-captain Wayne Wong acknowledged that the team had in some respects lucked its way to victory. It had placed first in its division during the summer session (when there are fewer teams and a more relaxed vibe overall), which allowed it to circumvent playoffs and go straight to the tournament. There were some much stronger teams at citywides, Wong said, but those teams mostly played against and eliminated each other, opening a path for his to win it all. Plus, it was 11 p.m. by the time the team's last player, Brian Hale, had to play his final match at citywides, more than twelve hours after the tournament began. "I won by a combo of me shooting pretty well and my opponent being drunk," Hale laughed.

Kickin' Like Bruce is made up of a group of old friends who grew up together in Chinatown. The team is all-Asian ("all Chinese and one Filipino")

A team of longtime friends. *Left to right:* Kickin' Like Bruce's Vegas-bound 2020–2021 lineup included Wayne "Bubba" Mui, Wayne Wong, Vincent "Bo" Lee, Jennifer Mui, Victor Mui, Cynthia Seid-Tang, and Lyn Panabi-Dumagpi. Not pictured is Brian Hale. (Courtesy of Ross Schaefer/Chicago Central APA.)

and everyone is between forty and fifty years of age. Several teammates went to elementary school together, some are married, and most live within a few blocks of each other. Hale was invited onto the team by his wife, who tragically passed away in 2018, leaving Hale to mourn her loss with his extended pool family.

Even if their citywides performance wasn't their best, there were plenty of exciting moments, and everyone on the team had a few standout shots that made them feel as though they contributed to the victory. The win felt especially good because it would be many of the teammates' first trip to the World Championships (if not Vegas itself), and the team had plans to meet even more friends in Sin City.

Wong, who came to City Pool Hall that evening from his new job at a Lexus dealership, joined the APA in 2011 and won a trip to Vegas in 2013 on his 8-Ball and 9-Ball teams and ended up playing pool for eleven days straight. He slept only three hours a night between playing and partying, which meant he ended up getting skunked in 8-Ball and not doing great in 9-Ball. "Eleven days is way too long," he said. "By the end of it, I was like, 'I can't take another day of this shit.'"

Wong advised that they take it easy party-wise this time, and everyone, now a bit older and wiser, agreed that they wanted to fully concentrate on the game. But it would be hard to shake the impulses honed in their pool-playing youth. Back in the day, Wong worked at the second iteration of a legendary Chicago pool room called Dragon Cue, on Wentworth Avenue and 28th Street. Bo Lee used to come by after the boss left for the night and the pair would shoot pool until the early hours of the morning.

Before YouTube and online forums existed, often the only way to get a real education in pool playing was to get your ass kicked by a high-caliber player. At Dragon Cue, Wong and Lee used to watch newer (or still un-humbled) players go up against the sharks and take a significant beating. The real serious guys would regularly play $500 games, and Hale once saw someone win more than $10,000 across a couple of matches. "I was nineteen or twenty at the time," he said. "I couldn't fathom what that [kind of money] meant." (Years later, Lee jumped at a chance to join Kickin' Like Bruce when a spot finally opened up. Despite their long history, he had to play his way onto the team to prove he could carry his weight.)

The friends drew on the lessons from this grittier world as they got more serious about the game, fitting in with their peers in more ways than one. "Some people—a lot of people—think I'm responsible for getting Dragon Cue shut down," said teammate and longtime friend Wayne "Bubba" Mui. Pool's reputation has always been colored by the extracurricular activities that accompany it, and as innocuous as the APA can seem, it is still home to players who cut their teeth playing a version of the game similar to that which once got pool banned by the state of Illinois.

As far as sports historians can tell, the game that would become pool was developed as an indoor version of a croquet-like outdoor lawn game, an idea supposedly brought back to Europe by Knights Templar after the Crusades in the eleventh century. The adapted tabletop game was a well-documented pastime among fifteenth-century European nobility, with the first recorded mention of a pool table said to be among the itemized belongings of King Louis XIV of France, "whose frequent stomach discomforts were thought to be quelled by the constant moving and stretching required at his billiard table."

Instead of cues, however, players used hooked staffs called "maces" to push balls through a wicket-like goal called a "port" and touch a pin called a "King" without knocking it over. There were pockets, but they were used to derail your opponent, not to gain points for yourself. The name *billiards* is said to originate with either the French word *bille* ("ball") or *billart*, the name for the wooden stick used to play the game. (There are ongoing debates about where precisely these terms came from and even what language they represent.) Early tables were humongous, some 6 ×12 feet, and weighed a literal ton, but they were gradually scaled down for the sake of convenience. Over time, cues were narrowed, rails were added to the sides of the playing field, and the game evolved so that in most cases sinking balls into pockets was the way to win.[2] The game quickly spread: *The Compleat Gamester*, an English rulebook from 1674, notes that there were "few Tones of note therein which hath not a publick Billiard-Table."

There's no way to know for sure who had the first table in North America,[3] but there are examples of ornate billiard tables built by American woodworkers in the 1700s (though inexperience with the game often meant that they were like the TJ Maxx version of the more elegant European tables). Public rooms devoted entirely to billiards appeared in the United States by the early 1800s, and diaries and travel journals record the presence of billiard tables hauled by wagon to obscure frontier outposts. George Washington and Abraham Lincoln were said to be huge fans of the game, while eighteenth-century

---

2. In 1587 Mary, Queen of Scots, noted in a letter that her billiards table was taken away during her imprisonment, and a rumor held that her decapitated body was wrapped in the table's velvet. The game is also mentioned in Shakespeare's *Antony and Cleopatra* (1600).

3. One historian, for example, claims that the game was introduced in the early 1600s by a Spanish family living in St. Augustine, Florida.

Virginia legislator William Byrd noted in his diary that, during one lovemaking session, "the flourish was performed on the billiard table."[4]

The name *pool* itself is said to come from the tables installed in the betting parlors of racetracks, which were known as "poolrooms" because that's where bets were pooled, and gambling was largely to thank for the popularity of pool in a growing Chicago. The game was particularly popular among what historians have called the city's "bachelor subculture," or the elevated number of single men in the city who immigrated and emigrated there to work in the steel, meatpacking, garment, and railroad industries. These men had to blow off steam somewhere, and bars and saloons with pool tables were accused of luring men away from the "quiet virtues of home and family" in favor of gambling, fighting, and drinking. "Either you're closing your eyes to a situation you do not wish to acknowledge or you are not aware of the caliber of disaster indicated by the presence of a pool table in your community," as Robert Preston sings in *The Music Man*.

Chicago certainly had its share of illicit gambling, as the city was known for its top-notch horse racing in the late nineteenth and early twentieth centuries, which funneled significant amounts of money into whatever political machine was in power. Groups of social reformers occasionally gained enough traction to pressure politicians to crack down on immoral activities, including those involving racetracks and underground boxing, and pool fans had to wonder if their sport was next.

But pool had also always been played outside the more scabrous environments, and that was true in Chicago as well. The popularity of sports as a recreational activity grew enormously in the second half of the nineteenth century as immigrant populations exchanged games, work reforms led to more leisure time (for some, at least), and the telegraph enabled fans to stay engaged with the newly formed professional leagues. Pool, fans of the game said, was just as virtuous as any sporting interest—it instilled critical thinking, discipline, and self-reliance; moreover, it was an Americanizing force that should be encouraged in a city such as Chicago, whose population by 1890 was 79 percent foreign-born or children of immigrants.

Leaning into the earning potential of the more "refined" side of the sport, pool halls were built or revamped to allow patrons to play pool "free

---

4. The game of 8-Ball is a relatively recent development that has become what most people think of first when pool is mentioned. The games played in the nineteenth and early twentieth centuries were substantially different with regard to rules and strategy, although they typically employed the same equipment. This is where the difference between *billiards* and *pool* is pronounced; while the two terms are often used interchangeably, aficionados are much pickier about how they refer to the type of game being played.

from disgusting associations." Foley's Palace Billiard Hall, run by Chicago billiard ace Tom Foley on Clark Street, was regarded as the "handsomest, best equipped, most thoroughly appointed establishment of the kind on the continent. . . . The hall is one of great magnitude, with nearly ten thousand square feet of floor, with high frescoed ceilings, like the ceilings of a church, and, but for the presence of the green cloth and billiard furniture, would present the aspect of a magnificent chamber of commerce." Many of these halls featured restaurants, bars, and even barbershops and humidors, all served by "attentive (and sometimes white-gloved) staff."

These halls hosted exhibition matches and well-paying tournaments that drew thousands of paying spectators and were covered extensively in the city's newspapers and homegrown periodicals such as *Billiards Magazine*. The events were sponsored by equipment manufacturers, thus providing a convenient way to showcase the equipment being used.[5] While the large prizes advertised in these tournaments were sometimes a marketing gimmick (the contestants didn't win thousands of dollars in a match but were more like actors or employees who were paid a flat fee for their appearance) tournaments sponsored by manufacturers and trade groups tended to distribute prizes more honestly than less scrupulous organizers, helping establish pool as a viable and well-attended sporting enterprise. Soon enough, Chicago became a national pool hotspot known for its "overwhelming industry dominance and influence in the realm of tournaments and championships." As the late Chicago pool historian D. B. Bond writes, "As a championship player, you certainly wanted to prove yourself in New York. You had to win in New York. But none of that mattered unless you won in Chicago too."

Tournament players became mini-celebrities in their own right, and this helped popularize the idea of the tuxedo-clad player who takes a sip from a cocktail while playing a gentlemanly (if not still cutthroat) game. These matches and tournaments were the subject of major coverage in newspapers, players appeared on trading cards that came with cigarettes, and top-notch players went overseas to entertain troops. Following World War II, returning veterans flocked to pool halls to relive their adventures on military bases, but the light of these glamorous days slowly dimmed as interest in the sport waned and other games and activities rose up to replace it (bowling had one of its heydays as pool's faded), bringing an end to the era of the game's greatest renown by the 1950s.

---

5. Little is different today when it comes to sponsorships: Photos from the time show hand-painted wooden advertisements lining the court or playing area.

Pool's popularity boomed in the 1960s thanks in large part to the release of the iconic 1961 film *The Hustler*, starring Paul Newman and Jackie Gleason. The film, which portrayed underground pool as a dangerous, high-stakes, but alluring game, drew more people out to shoot—if more for fun than to live the full hustler life. Chicago was host to many amateur and professional tournaments during this time, and another surge in interest followed the release of *The Color of Money*, the 1986 sequel to *The Hustler*, about the misadventures of a cocky 9-Baller played by Tom Cruise. Many of my relatives and friends' parents bought pool tables during this time, but the game's popularity waned in the 1990s and early 2000s, and a lot of these tables ended up becoming storage places for debris that collected in basements. But the continuing growth of the APA leagues, the influence of social media, and the perennial appeal of a group-based recreational activity has led to a noticeable uptick in pool playing and the opening of cool new pool bars over the past decade or so.

The tradition of hard-knock underground pool shooting always endured regardless of the level of mainstream interest. Far from the glitz of the big public halls meant for civilians, hardcore players gambled and hustled in smoky, windowless dives where rats fell out of the ceiling onto tables that were patched with tape and that used ashtrays for pockets. "I once played in an all–Puerto-Rican spot in Chicago that was in a cement floor basement," recalled the notorious Chicago hustler Freddy "The Beard" Bentivegna. "The entrance was a trap door and you had to climb down a portable ladder. It had two bar tables and nobody spoke English. Once you were in, the ladder was removed." It wasn't just locals who played in these dives. As old-school road warrior and author Jay Helfert explained, in the 1960s and '70s, there were a few hundred roadmen criss-crossing the country with their little black books full of addresses of bars and pool halls in towns big and small.

This is the world of pool that gave rise to Chicago players with names such as Bugs Rucker, Mexican Johnny, Jet Johnson, and Piggy Banks Rogers, players who helped give the city its reputation with their specialties and tabletop personalities. These guys played long and hard, and many only played pool for a living. Making $50 a day was considered a success, Helfert said—hotels were $15 a night, gas was fifty cents a gallon, and you could eat very well for $10 a day—but it was also very easy to be down on your luck. Almost all of them had times when they were busted and broke, sometimes having to sleep under pool tables until they got back on their feet. The Beard said he once turned down someone's request to at least leave him with bus fare home because he wanted to teach him the same lesson he'd learned years earlier. "If I'm gambling with you for big money, I'm not going to be friendly, OK? I want you to fear me," the Beard said. "I want to kill you. I want to eat your eyeballs, OK? That's how you think."

As unpredictable and troublesome as this world could be, not having to submit to the strictures of a 9-to-5 job was very appealing, the exhilarating action pushing people to incredible ends. At one point, despite not having anywhere close to the money he was betting, Bentivegna posed as an eccentric billionaire and won almost a million dollars against a high-stakes gambler so notorious that one casino had special $25,000 chips only he could use. But his opponent caught on, and the Beard was only able to collect about $200,000 of his winnings.

"I don't want to say all hustlers are degenerate gamblers, but hustlers like to bet on a lot of things," said the Beard's daughter Cat Adami, whose personal rebellion was being a straight-A student and not playing pool. "I was at a pool hall when I was five and my brother was two-and-a-half and a guy who lost a match got angry at dad and beat him up."

Dragon Cue, where members of Kickin' Like Bruce used to play, fit into this pantheon of hustlers and dives. That's where Wayne Mui, a few years younger than his friends and teammates, was taken under their wing.

"My parents owned a restaurant at the time that closed at 3 a.m. As long as I left Dragon Cue by 2:50 I could get home before they got there and they thought I was in all night," Mui said one evening over a club sandwich at City Pool Hall. "I would wake up at 6:30 and go to Brian's and sleep 'til 1 in the afternoon," gesturing at his teammate Brian Hale, who mimed shame for his role in helping him skip school. "The pool hall opened at 2 and we'd go right there or play basketball."

Mui and his friends made up a small crew that, like many others throughout their neighborhood, kept an eye on things to make sure people from other parts of town didn't come in and try to mess with Chinatown. They weren't gangs as much as block watch crews, though personalities often clashed when they congregated at Dragon Cue.

"I was a hothead when I was younger and started a lot of fights there," Mui said. "We're talking, like, once a week. I was sixteen, seventeen, just a dumb kid. The fights weren't about anything, I had nothing to prove, but a few of them got really serious, like, gunshot-serious."

Hale confirmed this, again not especially proudly, and elaborated on one incident.

Mui thought that a man he was playing was laughing at or taunting him, so he went over and slapped him so hard he banged his head into the wall. A bunch of people jumped up to fight but got talked down. One side suggested that Mui was supposed to pour tea for his opponent as an apology. "Yo, fuck that," Mui said, and everyone jumped up again. The fight spilled out into the parking lot and turned into a massive brawl that in some retellings involved more than sixty people. Word got out and people started avoiding Dragon Cue because they didn't want to get caught up in such a maelstrom, which purportedly led to the hall's shutting its doors.

Mui's cue stayed in the back of his closet for years after he got married and became a father, but he joined the APA a few years back and has been able to play more pool now that his child is older. His approach to the game has matured as he has. He's personally more patient, a bit mellower than before; the heightened competition of league play provides enough tension to scratch the itch that once propelled him forward but was low-key enough not to draw him back into that earlier mindset.

Back at City Pool Hall, the game Mui was watching as he ate his sandwich came to a close. He pushed his plate away, wiped his hands with a napkin, and excused himself from the conversation. He and his opponent lagged, balls cracked loudly, and two of Mui's balls went right into pockets. There was clearly still an edge to his game.

"You lucky muddafucka, you! You muthafucka! You fuckin' muthafucka!" his opponent muttered, sounding like Joe Pesci.

Wayne Wong observed the game from a nearby table. He, too, appreciated the chance to hang out with his friends—he said he doesn't want to be on a team if it's not with them—but the game was, of course, inherently competitive: You simply have more fun when you win.

"In Vegas," he said, "if we get knocked out early, it's going to be a little bit embarrassing."

CHAPTER 4

The Skills of a Chess Player and the Touch of a Pianist

The Billiard Men and a Few Words on Technique

> This is my [cue]. There are many like it, but this one is mine. My [cue] is my best friend. It is my life. I must master it as I must master my life. Without me, my [cue] is useless. Without my [cue], I am useless. I must fire my [cue] true. I must shoot straighter than my enemy who is trying to [beat] me. I must shoot him before he shoots me.
>
> —An adaptation of the Rifleman's Creed

If you were to play a drinking game in which you take a shot every time a henchman is playing pool in a crime movie, you'd probably get a decent buzz going before the movie was over. But while playing pool is often a sign that someone is plotting something bad (or at least gets the point across that the criminal is a calculating individual) there are a number of movies about pool for pool's sake. The best-known pool movies are unquestionably 1961's *The Hustler* and its 1986 sequel *The Color of Money*.

The Hustler tells the story of "Fast" Eddie Felson, played by Paul Newman, who goes through various trials and tribulations as a road hustler trying to redeem himself after a brutal loss. *The Color of Money* picks up twenty-five years later, with Felson now a bootleg liquor salesman in Chicago who has put his hustling days behind him. But when he sees the talented but arrogant Vincent (Tom Cruise), he begins teaching Vincent and his girlfriend the proper way to hustle. From there the movie is a series of tough life lessons learned from, with Felson and Vincent ultimately facing each other in a tournament showdown.

Other pool movies include *The Player* (1971), which stars real-life pool player Minnesota Fats; *Chalk* (1996), the story of a man playing to win money to help his stepfather who has throat cancer; and *Poolhall Junkies* (2002), which was co-written and directed by star Mars Callahan and is based on his own experiences as a pool player. Unfortunately, *The Player* was shown only in private screenings and a print doesn't seem to exist,[1] and the other films are considered terrible even by pool players. *Chalk* was called "insulting and outrageous," and *Poolhall Junkies* is widely derided largely because of Callahan's acting choices, which made it akin to watching someone unintentionally play an over-the-top satire of Ben Affleck for an entire movie. "Who the fuck did they get as a consultant on this?" asked Chicago APA player Eddie May, noting the latter movie's lack of attention to detail. "No professional plays with a $50 cue." (It was similarly unclear whom the producers consulted for the 2019 Chinese movie *Metal Billiards*, in which the main character is an "industrial design student who creates a robotic arm that he uses to advantage his billiards game and ultimately avenge his father.")

Although *The Hustler* may seem a little slow and disjointed to today's viewers, the movie and its sequel were nominated for Academy Awards[2] and inspired the aforementioned upswing in the sale of pool tables and overall interest in the sport.

Ironically, *The Hustler* is actually quite a grim movie. The story is a character study of Felson, whose dalliances in the "perverted, twisted, and crippled" world of hustlers results in his thumbs being broken by vengeful toughs and his girlfriend committing suicide when it's clear he'll never learn his lesson about the perils of pride. While there is some amount of lowlife glamor, the movie makes it clear that pool hustling is a dangerous and unrewarding lifestyle that can break even the most talented and fearless man.[3]

References to the characters and the story are common in the pool world,[4] but players in Chicago don't have to go far to immerse themselves in the atmosphere of those movies, because it's still possible to play in some of the

---

1. According to billiardsmovies.com, the location of a single print of the film is among the world's greatest unresolved mysteries along with the "identity of the Zodiac serial killer, the location of the Bermuda Triangle, and the translation of the Voynich Manuscript."

2. Newman won his only Oscar for his role as the aged Felson in *The Color of Money*.

3. According to critic Eric San Juan, *The Color of Money* was its own kind of redemption for director Martin Scorsese, who finally found success after a series of box office bombs.

4. Legendary player-hustler Rudolf Walderone, a.k.a. Minnesota Fats, took his name from one of the antagonists in *The Hustler*, retconning the nickname to have originated with him and parlaying his renown into sponsorship deals and essentially being the public face of pool.

halls that directly inspired or were featured in the films. Bennington's, a hall seen in *The Hustler*, was based on Bensinger's, a legendary three-story Chicago joint on Clark and Diversey, and *The Color of Money* was almost shot on location at Marie's Golden Cue at 3241 West Montrose. Lore has it that Marie's owners fixed the place up when they learned *Color's* producers were location scouting, only to have director Martin Scorsese declare the place too clean and walk right back out.

Chris's Billiards, on the other hand, was featured in *The Color of Money* likely *because* of its dirt. Located at 4637 North Milwaukee Avenue in Jefferson Park, Chris's is the seventeen-thousand-square-foot second floor of an old warehouse that used to be a meat-processing facility. The place is uniformly dark and dank, with its tables lit by shaded fluorescent lights, and overall it has the same color palette as the first *Saw* movie, a sensation underscored by the thick flaps of plastic that hang in the doorways leading to the tables in adjoining rooms. The sign out front boasts "41 tables," and Chris's is one of the only places in Chicago with a proper carom billiards table, an enormous, pocketless table almost always occupied by older men speaking Spanish and betting long into the night. A well-stocked snack bar sits at the front of the room, the attendant working both the counter and the elevated front desk. For some reason the entire place is carpeted, and you can practically feel its character through your shoes. "There are places you'll stand where you can't lift your foot up," one player said. "I'm sure people have been murdered on that carpet."

The regular clientele at Chris's is almost exclusively male and skews at least thirty-five years of age, if not older. The diverse ethnicities and socioeconomic backgrounds reflect the makeup of Chicago, but there are plenty of people who fit the mold of someone you might expect to find at a pool hall. Most look as though they can handle a few drinks and are longtime smokers; a few are put together, like a well-dressed car salesman, while others look as if they're used to being down on their luck. Periodically a guy in polyester pants and an untucked undershirt might emerge bleary-eyed from a back room to break some bills or get a cup of burnt coffee from the hot plate. He'll grunt technical play-by-plays of the games he'd just lost to the man behind the counter, who, an avid player himself, will nod along sympathetically. His complaints made, the player will then walk heavily back through the plastic flaps to try to dig himself out of the night's hole.

Chris's lightens its vibe a bit with the APA 9-Ball league on Sunday afternoons. Shades are opened to let some light in, and sometimes pool-playing parents bring their kids and let them play elsewhere in the cavernous room. Teammates act like doting aunts and uncles as kids play in a corner and make forts out of a pile of old furniture, pieces of pool tables, and assorted carpet squares. "Who wants an ice cream?" one player asks, to a rapturous response. Treats were soon distributed—ice cream for the kids and bottles and cans for the adults.

The APA teams that play at Chris's are part of the Chicago APA league, which is distinct from Ross Schaefer's Chicago Central APA league but has the same schedule, rules, and goal of going to Vegas. The Chicago APA league encompasses the north and northwest sides of the city and is run by Brad Hall, a longtime Chicago shooter who knew a lot of the local legends from earlier eras. This league kept up a slightly more regular pace of play throughout the pandemic because the APA left it up to the local leagues to follow the social distancing and capacity guidance of their respective localities. Hall was able to "work within the system" of shutdowns and technical exceptions that allowed some non-food-serving pool halls (such as Chris's) to stay open. He also predetermined each night's playing order so players could play their matches one at a time in order to satisfy capacity limits. This meant that the teams that qualified for Vegas had a bit more table time under their belt than teams in other jurisdictions, not to mention that his league, like many of the larger APA leagues, has an extra layer of tournament play called the Tri-Cup between the session-ending playoffs and the citywides.

Among the teams playing in the Sunday 9-Ball league at Chris's is Mancha United, which includes a few members of an 8-Ball team called the Billiard Men, which made it through the Tri-Cup to qualify for the 2021 Citywides and are based out of a bar called Surge Billiards in the Albany Park neighborhood. Eli Mancha, captain of both Mancha United and the Billiard Men, and a few of his teammates were glad to be playing on as many teams as they could in preparation for citywides and, they hoped, beyond.

Soon enough, Mancha arrived at Chris's to play on the Sunday team. He did not come to the pool hall with kids in tow, as he has none of his own. He prefers that the only person he must take care of is himself, and it is this approach that has allowed him to focus on the things that have made him successful on the table and off.

Trim and stylish and looking younger than his forty-four years, Mancha is one of the people whose presence is such that a get-together might not seem complete until he arrives. He started playing pool as a child at his dad's house and was recruited to play on an APA team by a guy he now considers his pool mentor when Mancha moved to Chicago to become a hair stylist. He qualified for the Vegas tournament in his first year in the APA on a team made up of members of his immediate and extended family, and they wound up placing 105th of more than 700 teams. "My little brother is a 7," Mancha said. "He failed a semester at college to get that good." Mancha qualified three more times over the subsequent years across a variety of teams, and the seriousness with which he takes the game has only compounded over time.

The only other thing in Mancha's life that comes close to his obsession with pool is his work as a stylist. He opened Bang! salon in Wicker Park on North Milwaukee Avenue in 2007 and was named North American Hairstylist of the Year in 2011. Mancha's clients know he is a pool fanatic, and much of their chair talk is dedicated to updates on how his teams are doing and how the latest session is unfolding. Mancha often gives talks at hairstyling conferences or is flown in to teach at salons and schools around the country, including classes on specialized dyeing techniques and cutting wigs. He'd recently been doing more teaching than usual and had been jetting around to exotic locales such as . . . Manchester, New Hampshire. "Can someone please send me to Miami or L.A.?" he laughed.

Regardless of where and how he does it, Mancha loves to teach, and APA league nights were a chance for him to put the combined instincts of an instructor, mentor, business owner, and pool captain toward a real shot at victory. Whether at Surge or at Chris's, Mancha can typically be seen shuttling between the table where his team is playing and one of the open practice tables, coaching players and helping newer shooters get used to playing competitively. This could include playing a few games and analyzing each shot, lining up balls to shoot in succession, or positioning a ball far down the table to try to sink some longer shots. He's had to kick people off the team for not showing up consistently or getting too drunk, which is why he now takes a few hours to shoot with prospective teammates to make sure the chemistry works before offering them a place on the team. "They don't even have to be good," he said. "They just have to be cool."

While getting good at pool is a steep learning curve, the basic principles of the game are universal and replicable. Just as knowing a few basic chords on the guitar or spice combinations in the kitchen can endow you with surprising versatility, the same can be said of the fundamentals of pool.

A few weeks after the Sunday at Chris's, Mancha was going about his captainly duties at Surge Billiards, a newer pool hall/bar/coffee shop with muted, non-fluorescent lighting and noticeably clean carpeting that was the team's home base. The tables at Surge are covered with a vivid blue felt that seems electric in the dim light, and the whole vibe is classy but accessible, with Cuban fusion food available thanks to a small kitchen inside the establishment. It was Mancha who started the APA league at Surge, helping coordinate the first eight teams to play in the new hall.

As Mancha explained, consistency is key no matter which billiard game you're playing. It is very important for newer players to build up the muscle memory for good shooting technique as early as they can because even a slight variation in arm angle can drastically change how the tip interacts with the ball and then how the ball interacts with the balls or rails.

The best way to approach the table is to stand with your feet at a T in front of the table, not with both feet facing forward, he said. There should be a straight line that extends from the trajectory of your shot up through your stick under your chin and through your back arm. The stick should be held loosely but controlled and swing evenly like a pendulum, "moving forward and back, not chicken-winged out to the side." Most shots require not a solid whack but a much more measured (or even soft) technique.

Is It Called Billiards or Pool?

When people say *pool*, they generally mean 8-Ball or 9-Ball, or at least a game played with a cue ball and solid and striped balls, and the word *billiards* is used interchangeably or as a fancier way to refer to the sport. However, among aficionados (or players in countries where pool isn't the dominant game), billiards often refers to a specific set of cue sports that developed in parallel with but somewhat separately from pool.

The game we know as pool today went through several iterations over the centuries, and the dominant pool game likewise changed over the years as interests, trends, and ways of gambling evolved. Some of the most prominent billiards games that have been played over the past two hundred or so years include the following.

Bank Pool: A game in which players score points by potting balls into the pockets by banking them off the cushions, with specific rules regarding combinations and the 5 ball often being the key ball. (Chicago was historically known for its bank pool players.)

Bumper Pool: A tabletop game played on a rectangular table with toadstool-shaped bumpers arrayed in the middle of the table and a single pocket flanked by bumpers on each of the short sides of the table. Players use cue sticks to sink balls into their opponent's pockets.

Carom Billiards: A cue sport played on a pocketless table whose objective is to score points by hitting both the opponent's and your own cue ball, as well as the object ball, in a single shot.

Cutthroat (a.k.a. Elimination): Typically played with three players. Each player is assigned a group of balls (solid, striped, or black), and the objective is to eliminate the other players' balls while keeping your own group intact.

English Billiards: A cue sport played on a rectangular table with pockets involving the use of two cue balls and one red object ball in which players score points by potting balls and performing specific combinations.

One Pocket: A strategic game in which each player chooses one of the two corner pockets as his or her target and must sink all of his or her designated balls into that pocket to win.

Rotation (a.k.a. 61): In this game, players must sink balls in numerical order, starting with the 1 ball and aiming to reach a specific point total, often 61 points. The necessity of sinking balls in numerical order often requires making combination, bank, or otherwise challenging shots.

Snooker: A cue sport played on a pocketed rectangular table with twenty-one colored balls and a cue ball, in which players aim to score more points than their opponents by potting balls in a specific order.

Straight Pool (a.k.a. 14.1 Continuous): A more strategic and precise game in which players aim to reach a certain point total by potting balls in any order, with a focus on racking up as many points as possible.

Straight Rail (a.k.a. Straight Billiards): A simple and early form of carom billiards in which players scored points by hitting both object balls with at least one rail between them.

10-Ball: Similar to 9-Ball but played with ten numbered balls, and players must legally pocket the 10 ball to win.

Three-Cushion Billiards: A carom billiards game played on a pocketless table in which players aim to score points by making the cue ball contact at least three cushions before hitting the opponent's ball and the object ball.

But shooting is more than just how you use the cue; it's also about using the physics of the table to your advantage. Fortunately, learning this is a bit easier for players today because early in the game's history there were no prescribed dimensions governing the table's size. According to one manual, the playing surface of a pool table should be "somewhat longer than it is broad; Both length and width being left to your discretion." Eventually it was realized that uniform table sizes would make for a more standardized game, which in turn meant more players inclined to play competitively.

Today, pool tables come in one of three sizes. The smallest are "bar boxes," measuring 3.5 × 7 feet and so named because they're the most convenient size for bars. Tables that are 4 × 8 feet are usually found in homes, and tables 4.5 × 9 feet in size are considered professional size. Generally, bigger tables require longer shots and smaller tables have play based around balls grouped more closely together. Each brand of table has its own benefits and deficiencies, which astute players can readily identify. Diamond tables have fast felt and tighter pockets, for example, whereas Valley brand tables, the kind used in the APA World Championships, have bigger pockets. "It hurts a little more when you miss on those," Mancha said.

One of the game's most recognizable actions is chalking the end of a cue, and that's because chalk is a critical part of the game. Chalk—typically a mix of pulverized silica, glue, coloring agent, and an abrasive substance such as emery powder—is applied in order to increase friction between the tip and the ball, an additional moment of grip that helps make a shot all the more precise.[5] As one bit of wisdom holds, "Chalk should be applied like a beautiful woman applies her lipstick": You don't grind it on, you caress the tip into the bowl-shaped indentation so it's not compacted and slippery. Some players prefer specific brands or compositions, and most keep their chalk cube handy via keychain or a magnet in their pocket that keeps the cube stuck to the front of their pants.

In the early days, players used bare wooden cues to hit the ball, resulting in fairly clumsy shots, and the use of a padded cue tip was said to have been perfected by the Frenchman François Mingaud sometime in the late 1700s while in prison for being an "adventurer whose presence in society can only be dangerous." So promising was this innovation that he was said to have asked for more time in prison to continue his experiments. Aghast crowds claimed that the balls were "tormented by a devil" at the exhibitions he gave following his release, but today we know this form of possession is simply skilled use of the cue.

Early balls were made of ivory. Only four or five balls could be made from a single elephant tusk. Aside from the disgusting violence involved in obtaining the substance, one of the problems was that ivory is uniformly dense only when it comes from the center of the tusk, and the frequent collisions of pool balls created areas of unequal density that made them roll off-center. In the late nineteenth century, a table manufacturer offered $10,000 ($300,000 in 2025 dollars) to anyone who could come up with a substance that would make a better pool ball. The inventor John Wesly Hyatt attempted to use intense pressure to form balls from a mixture of nitrocellulose, camphor, and alcohol, but the material wasn't stable if it wasn't cured properly, and there

---

5. In the interest of not explaining the ins and outs of every kind of shot, the reader is advised to check out some guidebooks like APA commentator Ewa Laurance's *The Complete Idiot's Guide to Pool and Billiards*, which explains the mechanics of various shots and the techniques required to make them. There are also countless videos on YouTube showcasing every pool shot there is. Some of the most difficult shots are massé and jump shots, which require a sharp downward stab at the ball that can rip a table's felt. For this reason, a sign thumbtacked to a corkboard at City Pool Hall advises, "No massé or jump shots unless you are rated a 5 or above."

The Billiard Men 2020–2021 with citywides trophies ready to be awarded to victorious teams. *Left to right:* Ricardo Cagnetta, Jackson May, Christine Arce, Eli Mancha, Ryan Morse, Pierre Kasiansky, and Ricky Torres. (Courtesy of Ross Schaefer/Chicago Central APA.)

were many accounts of balls exploding on the table. Bakelite, the predecessor of plastic, became the preferred substance for pool balls when it was invented in 1907, and today the majority of pool balls are made of phenolic resin, essentially updated Bakelite. Unlike bowling balls, which have different layers and a separate core, pool balls are made of the same material inside and out.

For his shooting cue Mancha uses a Lucassi butt with a carbon fiber Predator shaft, and for his breaking cue a limited-edition Viking butt and a shaft with a harder tip. A really good cue will cost a few hundred dollars, while top-shelf cues, handcrafted by masters of high-end materials and with intricate inlays, grips, and personalized embellishments, can cost thousands. As with any quality item, the difference between average and expensive sticks is quite apparent, the feel and craftsmanship making it seem as though it should indeed cost more, but most shooters advise that if you spend anything above $500 you're paying for clout. (One player told me he knows someone whose "income comes from something you can't file taxes for" and launders his illicit earnings through the buying and selling of valuable cues.)

Most bar cues are machined from single pieces of wood because it is cheaper, but no serious players will use them if they don't have to. Two-piece cues were invented in the middle of the nineteenth century, and the innovation wasn't just for the sake of portability. Splitting the cue cuts down on how far vibrations travel through the shaft, helping players make more accurate shots. Carbon fiber shafts are currently popular because they are the most vibration-resistant stick out there, and, as one player told me, helps with other issues, like the ball's squirt.

"I'm sorry, the squirt?" I asked.

Yes, the squirt, he said, apparently not seeing why the term was funny. When I looked it up later, I found that the ball's squirt is the "angular displacement of the cue ball's path away from the cue stroking direction caused by the use of sidespin," yet another example of the subtleties players must consider when taking their shots.

Some people say that experience with other sports that use small balls gives new pool players an advantage because people who play golf, ping-pong, tennis—"shit, even squash"—are familiar with manipulating objects across a plane and already have heightened hand-eye coordination. Many players say it's easier to improve if you start playing at a young age, when your mind is eager to absorb new things and you're less distracted by reality, but that's certainly not a requirement; many players pick up the game later in life and excel in ways they'd never realized they could. I knew one player who was a national grandmaster in chess who traded an equally accomplished pool player for lessons, with both quickly becoming great in their new pursuits.

A pool player's skill comes from putting all this knowledge together, and a good league player knows how to do all of this while also contributing to the broader strategy of team play. That means trying hard, having a willingness to learn, maintaining your chops, and being conscientious of the time and effort everyone else is putting into the game. "I'm passionate about what I like, and my credibility means a lot," Mancha said as he worked the room at Surge.

At that, he beckoned teammate Jon Ruiz, who was simultaneously working as a bartender, to ask him if his time off had been approved. The time had finally come: The Billiard Men would be competing at citywides, the long-awaited showdown for the Chicago APA league the following weekend.

"You know we really need you to be there," Mancha said.

"What's the schedule?" Ruiz asked.

"Schedule? There is no schedule. We need you there Saturday and Sunday at 9 in the morning 'til at least 7 at night, if not longer. Just plan to be there all day."

A pained smile flashed across Ruiz's face at the prospect of spending two nights in a row going out to the suburbs (and using time off from work to do so), but he knew what choice he was expected to make. As part of the team, he was indeed going to make it.

CHAPTER 5

A Forbidden Enchantment
The BB Cues and the Chicago Central APA Women's League

The BB Cues earned the chance to represent the Chicago Central APA's women's league at the 2020–2021 World Pool Championships in the summer of 2019, about as far back as it was possible to go in order to be included in the rescheduled 2020–2021 citywides.[1]

"It was a really close finals," said BB Cues founder and team captain Adina Fried. "Me and Janet [her opponent in the finals] went back and forth each game. It was really exciting to be there."

Their victory came when the women's league was still a traveling league, with teams rotating across three bars in central Chicago week to week. In the post-COVID period, the league was now headquartered in Surge Billiards in Logan Square, the sister location to the Surge Billiards in Albany Park that hosts the Billiard Men. Fried had long been pulling double duty: She captained her own team and played on others but was also the founder and organizer of the Chicago Central APA women's league itself. The women's league is not as populous as its co-ed counterpart—after the COVID gap the team count went from nine to six—but Fried says she's proud that she can provide women with an encouraging, competitive environment in which to learn the game, an option often unavailable in smaller leagues without the population to sustain a dedicated women's group.

---

1. Ordinarily, the APA Women's Championship is held at the fall World Pool Championships, but in 2021, on account of COVID, they were held at the APA Poolplayer Championships, which took place August 3–14. For ease of narration and because the location and set-up are the same for both events, the BB Cues' participation in the tournament will be discussed as if all Chicago teams discussed in this book were competing at the same event.

The BB Cues, Vegas-bound champions of the Chicago Central APA women's league. *Left to right:* Vivian Ramos (a pseudonym), Christine Degrange, Adina Fried, and Teresa Jimmerson. Not pictured is Allison Lewis. (Courtesy of Ross Schaefer/Chicago Central APA.)

Fried is originally from New Jersey and aside from pool is the manager of a prominent Chicago florist and at the time was working on launching her own floral supply business. Customers can be incredibly demanding given the important events for which flowers usually are bought, and the challenges of managing such a challenging business helped sharpen the skills she uses in her role as a local pool influencer. "I saw an episode of *Grey's Anatomy* with a character who was a florist. That's the only time I've seen the plight of a florist acknowledged!" she said. Fried has been playing pool since she was young, though the table at her parents' house was warped and the ball returns didn't work. When she decided to move in with her fiancé Eddie May, a well-connected pool player she met at City Pool Hall, it was hard to find a place to live that could accommodate their eight-foot table, because it is recommended that a table have five feet of unencumbered space around each side. Thus, their table is in storage until they are able to find a seven-footer to use at home.

"I pay $60 a month for a storage unit for the table—there's nothing else in it," she said. "We can't own two pool tables. That would be insane."

Fried was introduced to the APA years earlier by the ex-partner with whom she'd moved to Chicago and quickly found herself obsessed with playing league pool. A few years later she was on a team that made it to the Las Vegas championships and placed 64th of 267 teams, but it turned out her boyfriend spent all their funds on gambling and they barely had the money to make it through the week. Her interest in pool outlasted the relationship and has proved to be far more enchanting, and her continued involvement eventually led to her running the women's league and helming her own team.

Nearby, teammate Vivian Ramos[2] assembled her cue.

"I'm really competitive. If we're walking on the sidewalk and you're walking faster than me, I'll try to catch up," she said.

A chief risk officer at an insurance company, Ramos was first up at the 2019 citywides and lost her match, a fact she related with an expression of genuine guilt. Her teammates made up for it by cleaning house afterwards, but she clearly still bore the loss quite heavily and, speaking to the middle distance, vowed to do better in Vegas.

Most of the BB Cues had previously been to Vegas for reasons both personal and pool-related, but it would be the first time Ramos had ever been there. She'd avoided going there on vacation because she wanted her first experience to be with her team. "Pool is my outlet, my social environment. All my closest friends I've met through pool," she said. "Almost everything we do ends up revolving around a pool table—going to bars, people's houses with pool tables—that's what we do."

Pool was also a way for Ramos to cope with the constant disappointment of trying to buy a house in Chicago. She was especially preoccupied one evening while shooting at Surge, constantly stepping away from the table to check her phone. Her shoulders sank after one call, and she stood facing the wall as she took a moment for herself. It was the seventh time her offer had evaporated. Someone swooped in at the last moment and made an insurmountably high cash offer. "I just want a house, a yard," she said with a sigh.

The 2020–2021 BB Cues lineup also included Teresa Jimmerson, Christine Degrange, who'd qualified for Las Vegas that year on no fewer than four separate teams, and Alison Lewis, who had won trips to the World Championships on various teams every year since 2010, save for 2020 and the year her son was born. She joined the BB Cues when one of the original qualifying players couldn't make it to Vegas. "I'm always excited to go," Lewis said. "I'm on multiple teams at the same time. Adina said she needed people on the team she wanted to go to Vegas, and I was honored to do so."

As it happened, a women's team from Chicago called the Apocalypsticks would be going to Vegas in 2021 as well and would be defending the women's championship title they'd earned in 2019. Fried knew that a potential Chicago versus Chicago matchup would be both exciting and nerve-wracking because it was sure to be closely watched back home. "The Chicago pool community

---

2. A pseudonym.

is not that big," she said. "If a team gets deep [in the tournament], players from Chicago are invested."

Fried ranks as a 4 in the APA, and she tries to keep her goals modest to counterbalance the tension of the game. First, she concentrates on doing well in an evening, then in the league tournament, then at citywides, trying to stay in the moment to avoid getting bent out of shape about games she hadn't played yet. It doesn't take much for Fried to get excited, however, her mock exasperation turning to real exasperation as the stakes get higher, and she's known to blow off steam by dancing effusively in her own world next to the table before getting back down to business.

Speaking of exasperation, that's partly why the women's league exists: It can simply be exasperating playing as a woman in a league with hundreds of men. "There is lots of peacocking going on" in the pool scene, Fried said, at times giving the average hall a "school cafeteria" atmosphere that has made the women's league an especially welcoming alternative, an encouraging but serious place for women to practice their craft.

As many women explained, a female captain's knowledge of APA rules might be questioned or ignored in a way it would not be with her male counterparts. Captains sometimes pit women against women during league play, either unconsciously or to ensure that none of the team's male players is beaten by a girl. Even though it adds significant time to her commute, one player said she often goes home to change into baggier clothes so she doesn't have to deal with men commenting about bare shoulders or the length of her skirt (or the very fact that she was wearing a skirt). Another woman said she was genuinely scared about what would happen if a pool player known for his gross, aggressive behavior found out she was one of the many people who'd reported him for harassment, especially because he also happened to be a cop.

One evening I was talking with a player at City Pool Hall, and he in turn introduced me to his teammate, who had just walked over after finishing his match. "I told him, 'I'm here to teach you two things,'" the teammate said of the man who introduced us. "'How to shoot pool, and how to pull pussy!'" Asked how his match had gone, he cackled, "I was like R. Kelly. I violated them!" pumping his arm up and down in a crude gesture. It was a bold way to behave around someone you met seconds earlier. How much crasser would he have been if he *really* felt comfortable with me, or if I were a woman he was trying to "impress"? On the other hand, one woman said playing pool is a good way to determine a date's character and emotional maturity—anyone who got unduly upset or whiny if she beat them was not worth her time, for, what did this say about how he'd act in real life about a real issue?

While the pool scene is, of course, not universally uncomfortable for women (with many women saying the years or decades they've spent in league pool were among the most rewarding commitments of their lives), pool has been a predominantly male sport from its inception and carries the same patriarchal baggage as most aspects of our present reality do.

In the early days women were sometimes obligated to use a mace, the game's original broad-headed hooked implement, out of concern that a woman using a modern cue would rip the table's felt. Social expectations meant that women who did venture into the world of billiards often faced skepticism and prejudice and had their abilities and motivations questioned. This in turn led to a lack of inclusion in professional tournaments and leagues, creating a historical dearth of role models for aspiring female players and perpetuating the notion that cue sports were a man's domain. As scholar Kenneth Cohen put it, the "protection of women's innate virtue required their abstention from public tables," their delicate constitutions unable to handle the riff-raff associated with such places. When women did play, it tended to be in homes or private game rooms that minimized contact between "honest people" and the "underground universe."

These early restrictions on who could play were, of course, not based on any inherent difference in ability but rather on the insecurities of crybaby male players.[3] Though women had to work twice as hard as men to earn any kind of respect, bringing more women into the sport was eventually considered a way to improve the game's reputation (alongside "installing carpets and bright lights and pastel colors, curbing obscene language, [and] getting rid of hustlers and hoodlums and alcoholics"). Such changes slowly took place starting in the late 1800s, with the opening of one new pool room at the time said to have been "thronged by the light feet of a thousand fair women, to whom billiards had heretofore been a mystery or a forbidden enchantment." While it would still be discouraged for women to visit certain pool establishments or behave in certain ways, it was no longer shocking that a woman would want to play or that she would be able to play in public under the same rules that men did.

Besides, there have always been incredible female shooters, including Ruth McGinnis, who logged twenty-eight thousand miles per year traveling around the country to play pool starting in the 1930s, and the members of Chicago's first modern women's league, which was said to have been formed in 1967 after a few women began hanging out in a pool hall to stave off going stir crazy from being snowed in by that year's legendary blizzard. One of the most recognizable professional pool players of all time (and one of the APA's professional

---

3. One male player made the case that the difference in pelvic physics meant that men could make stronger breaks, but beyond that, he said, there is no observable difference in overall ability between the sexes.

instructors and spokespeople) is Jeanette "The Black Widow" Lee, a former New York City waitress who mastered the game despite having scoliosis ("I'm always going to break balls," she's been known to say), while Ewa Laurence, pool personality, author, and professional shooter for more than thirty years, is the other half of the pair doing live commentary of the finals matches at the World Pool Championships. The Women's Professional Billiard Association, founded in 1976, hosts a series of tournaments across the United States each year, and some of the players making the most money in pool today are Chinese women. Many players, pro and amateur alike, have expressed an interest in an "Open" category in professional competition to show once and for all that there is no difference between the sexes as to who can excel in pool. It's also important to note, said Nicole, a shooter in the Chicago women's league, that one of the teams in the league is called the Velvet Tacos, a female analogue to the endless puns about sticks and balls employed in the sport.[4]

Fried sometimes has to address accusations that she plays favorites or stacks her team with the best players ("Go out and make your own team!" she says in response) but her biggest issue is that she doesn't get paid for her work, a slight made worse by what she perceived as the APA's lack of serious interest in women's leagues. Women's teams have five players, versus eight for co-ed teams, and this, Fried theorized, meant less money and thus less incentive for the APA to focus on those leagues. She also knew that, given the rigors of running a league and running it for free, few people would be interested in taking over the duty in her absence.

"I don't look at [running the league] as a high-brow thing when I'm just trying to play. Sometimes I want to walk away, but then the [women's] league would go away," she said. "Thinking about what the space means and the effort I've already put into it, then yes, it does make it political. It's a great community for women and that makes me feel really good about what I do."

Just as Eli Mancha coached his team at the other Surge, it was Fried's job to transmit the same knowledge of the table, something she was happy to do for the women early in their pool journeys. Between watching her team playing and filling me in on her history and vision, Fried and a teammate would head over to an open table to practice. "You're stripes. What do you do?" she asked after setting up the balls like a chess problem. An intense consultation followed, with lots of pointing and gesticulating. The student soon sank a ball, the table was reset, and the BB Cues prepared to take their game to Vegas and showcase the serious capabilities of Chicago's women's league.

---

4. She also said she has a cue that looks like a cane and telescopes out from the bottom. "It was from my grandpa. He was kind of a scumbag but it's cool to have it."

CHAPTER 6

The Underground Arena
Waking and Breaking in Chicago's Small Bars

> He played at a good pace. He was polite. He was
> intelligent in conversation. He had a good sense of
> fairness. [He] had guts and gamble. He played hard.
> —Blog entry memorializing a player who
> exemplified the perfect opponent

If there were to be a monument constructed honoring the titans of U.S. billiards, a man named Tom Foley with his impressive 1800s mustache would be one of the monument's huge carved heads.

Born in 1842 in rural Ireland, Foley was "deported for family reasons" and came to the United States when he was six years old. At thirteen he began working at a billiard hall and within three years was a formidable player who "never lost a match of importance." He would go on to open a number of billiard halls in Chicago and St. Paul, refine and standardize the rules of play on the national scale, organize tournaments that drew substantial crowds, and overall serve as a tireless ambassador who greatly popularized the sport.

The "inherent ability of the Irishman to swing a club, be it a shillelagh or a hurling stick, may have had some influence on young Foley in the adoption of his chosen profession," as one newspaper put it. Given that Damo Moloney, co-founder of the Chicago Central APA team Wake and Break, is himself an Irishman, I asked if he believed that his inherent ability to swing a shillelagh was a factor in his pool game. No, he laughed, he never thought of it that way, but he did bring a different kind of Irish influence to Chicago.

Moloney works as a chef at The Kerryman, "Chicago's liveliest" Irish bar, which occupies a former punk and metal concert venue. He grew up in rural Ireland in a neighborhood that consisted of five houses sharing a plot of land. His family was the first to get flush toilets and plumbing, though this was still in an outhouse, he pointed out. He was always interested in cooking and would sneak some spices into the dishes his parents prepared, and he parlayed this culinary interest into a college scholarship, going to cooking school and deepening his interest in pool. He was hired as a chef in 2005 and has made his home in Chicago since then, eventually being recruited by team co-founders Jay Vatanagul and Sonia Aujla to play on Wake and Break.

Moloney is well regarded in his field for preparing high-quality traditional Irish foods and typically appears on a local news station each year to give a bit of information about Irish cuisine. One evening, as Wake and Break were playing a league match at Black Hole, their home bar, Moloney recalled once telling a news anchor off-air that corned beef and cabbage is not an Irish dish but in fact an American invention. He suggested that the host not ask him about this during the interview because he didn't want to burst anyone's bubble, but as soon as the taping began, the host said, "You were just telling me that corned beef and cabbage is not an Irish tradition—can you expand on that?" Moloney laughed at being put on the spot but was able to assuage any disappointment by noting that the dish was based on Irish cured pork, which was cheaper than beef but didn't change the fundamental idea of the dish. Moloney could roll with the punches, and thinking on his feet and not caving under pressure was certainly a set of skills he employed on the pool table.

Wake and Break shook off the cobwebs of a pandemic-era pool year and came back to win a trip to Las Vegas. *Left to right:* Damo Moloney, Oscar Sandoval, Jutichai Vatanagul, Jesus Perez, and Sonia Aujla. Not pictured are Matt Rink, Jorge Mora, and Owen Tracy Bacucang. (Courtesy of Ross Schaefer/Chicago Central APA.)

As part of the Chicago Central APA traveling league, Wake and Break's regular session games rotate among a series of small area bars. They include Emporium, a barcade with several vintage arcade cabinets and pinball machines and a bar box table that's seen better days, Gold Star, a hole-in-the-wall bar said to be one of the most haunted bars in Chicago, and Black Hole, a wood-paneled and dimly lit spot on Division Street in Ukrainian Village that's a home away from home for the team. Having played together for years, the team members typically sit clustered around a few small tables they'd pushed together to the side of the lone pool table, the setting feeling like an underground boxing match as opposed to City Pool Hall's more arena-like ambiance. Sonia Aujla was just outside smoking a cigarette, looking through a circle she'd wiped in the steamy glass to watch Jay Vatanagul shoot.

On the whole, Wake and Break prefer playing in smaller bars. While most places hosting Chicago APA teams charge $7 per person per night for league play, City Pool Hall, for example, charges $13, and that adds up if you're playing there on multiple teams per week. In addition, anywhere you want to park near City Pool Hall requires using parking meters, which aren't cheap. Conversely, many of the smaller bars such as Black Hole or the Surge Billiards are generally less expensive, are near residential streets with free and unrestricted parking, and overall have a more laid-back vibe.

Team captain Jay Vatanagul has a natural friendliness that makes him one of those people anyone can get along with. Born and raised in Chicago, he grew up on the early internet and credits not ancestral ability to swing a stick but rather Yahoo chat rooms with expanding his interest in pool. He learned a lot about the game's fundamentals this way and eventually tried his hand at replicating cool shots he saw in YouTube videos. If playing on a real table wasn't possible, Vatanagul practiced on a pool app on his phone—the geometry and physics were surprisingly accurate and could at the very least help players understand how to set up shots and how balls move. (Many players said pool apps were genuinely a good way to learn the game.) The only superstition that factors into his game is a small Deadpool figurine he uses as a pocket marker, and he's always been receptive to new ideas such as trying a pool glove, which he'd only started doing a few months before the team's winning performance that humid weekend of the 2021 citywides.

Vatanagul's approach to taking players to the next level is to be "competitive but encouraging," and the team is known for being a particularly pleasant group. "Jay and Sonia are great people to follow because (1) they're genuinely good people, (2) they're strong competitors, and (3) they know how to coach," said Carla, a friend hanging out nearby. She'd wanted to be on Wake and Break forever for this reason, and had even kept score for the team for a season just so she could spend more time with them. She was "overjoyed" when she was asked to join Kick Push, their Thursday team, which plays at Nick's Billiard Academy, a long-standing hall on Pulaski Road in Albany Park.[1]

But even a relatively chill team such as Wake and Break sometimes has to deal with unexpected personnel issues. There were members who took the game too seriously in an unhealthy way, snapping at teammates, getting in opponents' faces, and generally being a liability you had to walk on eggshells around.[2]

Once, in a game against an older iteration of Wake and Break, an opposing player set a cube of chalk down next to the pocket in which she intended to sink the 8 ball. Shooters are required to mark their pocket on the final shot so there are no misunderstandings about which pocket is being called (hence pocket markers such as Vatanagul's Deadpool figurine), and it's recommended that you don't use a cube of chalk for this purpose because it could easily be confused with the many other cubes on the table. When the player sank the ball and won, a player on Wake and Break completely freaked out at the alleged technical violation and made a very public display of his frustrations. Everyone on both teams saw what pocket she intended and accepted the way she called it, and the embarrassing outburst led to the man's being asked to leave the team.

On the extreme end of the player behavior spectrum, one player (not on Wake and Break) told me how the new girlfriend of her ex-boyfriend confronted her in a parking lot, and the pair took turns pushing each other up against walls and cars. The aggrieved player was almost beside herself with desire to play her enemy in an upcoming tournament, saying that beating her in a match on the pool table would be much more satisfying than a physical fight—and would show the ex what he'd walked out on. One of the craziest player encounters I heard about was related by Gregg Taylor, who described watching a man he knew who went from muttering to himself throughout a match to openly threatening his opponent, who was starting to lose his cool in return. "I said, 'Mike, you're old, you can't be acting like this, I'm not going to give you mouth-to-mouth,'" Taylor said. "The guy told me to

---

1. Nick's is a perfectly welcoming place located in an old shopping plaza. It feels like a cross between a bar and a VFW hall with a substantial grid of tables, although the first time I went there I watched someone lock himself in the ATM vestibule of an adjoining bank and completely destroy it.

2. This, of course is, not exclusive to pool. I once played in a charity kickball game in college and was astounded by how quickly some of my teammates were ready to yell at others or get really bent out of shape if a bewildered volunteer referee didn't rule in my team's favor or a teammate appeared not to be trying hard enough.

shut the fuck up. Then he loses and he starts hitting himself in the head really hard, giving himself contusions. I've never seen anything like it. He was kicked out of the hall and I had to call him and tell him he's banned from my tournaments."

But the only difficulty Wake and Break had recently faced was trying to stay positive when the team wasn't doing well in the first few rounds at the 2021 citywides. A player on one of the opposing teams was known for his hijinks and tried to psych out Wake and Break, talking loudly to a teammate when his opponent was trying to shoot and then suddenly disappearing when it was his turn to play, ignoring his teammates' texts and calls. It was unclear whether this was part of the ruse or whether they actually didn't know where he was, but he showed up almost fifteen minutes later and then made a big show of excessively chalking his cue as if nothing had happened. But Wake and Break slapped the mind games aside and beat the team to make it to the next round.

"I've seen people rip into a teammate if they miss a shot or lose a game, but I don't want that negativity in the air," Vatanagul said. "The teams play each other every couple of weeks, so sportsmanship is important, but there's always that one person or one team who gets too serious. You have to keep an eye on them 'cause they might pull something."

As it happened, one of their final matches of the 2021 citywides was against the Island of Lost Souls, a team with my former Chalkie's Children teammates James Terronez and Valentin Isasi. Both had originally joined Chalkie's Children as a favor to Ross Schaefer, and Terronez said that team was still "in shambles" and couldn't keep a full roster together, which is why neither of them had rejoined after the pandemic. But they still took the game seriously with the Island of Lost Souls, a team that pre-dated Chalkie's Children and COVID-19 and in whose success they were much more invested. Terronez had moved to Illinois from Wisconsin but had just as long a commute as he had before, yet he happily kept up the routine of playing pool with the Lost Souls.

Damo Moloney would go on to knock out Terronez, and then Sonia Aujla was up. She'd rushed in from playing in a DuPage County tournament earlier that afternoon and greeted her teammates before going back outside to smoke, collect her thoughts, and get in the zone. She knew practically everyone at the earlier tournament and was exhausted by all the socializing she had to do and was glad to be playing at City Pool Hall, where she knew fewer people and wouldn't have to expend as much energy talking. Still, her left eye twitched constantly, a holdover from the earlier stress, but she, too, managed to knock out a win despite the fatigue.

At one point the Island's captain came up to give a coach to the player playing against Wake and Break's Oscar Sandoval, making sure to wear a facemask to obscure the directions he was giving. His opponent had recently been raised to a 6, giving Sandoval, also a 6, more of a challenge than he was expecting, and the tension visibly slid down Sandoval's face as he steadily gained the upper hand. Wake and Break would, of course, go on to win a trip to the 2020–2021 World Pool Championships when Vatanagul's opponent missed the critical (and critically easy) shot at the 8 ball not long after that.

Etiquette holds that teams should keep their exhortations to themselves during a game, and excessive celebrating can even cost you a match, like the infamous yelp that cost Howard Dean a presidential nomination. But that doesn't mean that the final victory doesn't warrant a celebration when it's all said and done, which is what Wake and Break did, cheering as a team and celebrating each teammate's contribution to hype each other up for the road ahead. Coming back together after the privations of the pandemic was a great feeling, and what better way to celebrate winning a trip to a major tournament with your teammates and friends? But by then it was late at night, and the employees of City Pool Hall were eager to go home. They turned out the lights during the victory photo session and ushered people out before they could collect their trophies. The experience underscored their appreciation for the hominess of their home bar.

Wake and Break was one of the most cohesive and friendly teams of those I'd gotten to know, and back at the Black Hole the team heartily encouraged Moloney as he got up to swing a shillelagh when it was his turn at the table. Their path to Vegas was secured, so they could afford to use the current season to refine their skills and not concentrate as hard on being the top team in their league.

As for Tom Foley, the legendary Chicago pool player and promoter, he would put his passions to work for another sport that was gaining momentum in the nineteenth century. Foley became business manager of the Chicago Base Ball Association, which sold shares to the public to fund the creation of a Chicago-based professional baseball team, scouting and signing the city's first nine professional ball players and developing a twelve-thousand–seat stadium at an old race track. The team's characteristic uniforms led them to become known as the Chicago White Stockings, and when the team moved, Foley started a new team on the city's north side—the Chicago Cubs.

From Foley's pioneering efforts in the nineteenth century to the modern-day camaraderie of Wake and Break, the spirit of competition has always been intertwined with the venues in which it unfolds. In addition to the wins that take people from Chicago to Las Vegas, I observed how the classic adage "A dumbass and his money are soon parted" holds true in dive bars and swanky modern halls alike—and that seeing that adage play out in real life is a deeply satisfying experience.

PART II

Pool, On the Table and Off

CHAPTER 7

The Hubris of the Uninitiated
Anatomy of a Slaughter

Physically cheating at pool is not easy to do. First, you'd have to gain access to a table to tamper with it before a game, but then your opponent would likely notice anything amiss with uneven felt or doctored balls, as might any of the many spectators. Thus, the easiest way for players to get around the lack of mechanical advantage is to game their opponent's psychology. This, in essence, is the art of hustling.

The classic hustle is to pretend to play badly in order to lure people into what they think is an easy bet, and then, when their guard is down, play at your actual ability level, crush them, and take their money. Pool "sharps" (later "sharks") were "deceiv[ing] unsuspecting gentlemen" in this way as early as the 1600s, and some of the earliest pool strategy books warned players to be on the lookout for these underhanded techniques when playing in unfamiliar pool rooms. But it was only a matter of time before a shark's reputation caught up with him and he was forced to move on to a new, unsuspecting location. This kind of player would "continually pass from one Prison to another 'til their lives are ended," according to one old-time observer who'd no doubt been pummeled by sharks himself.

Sometimes hustlers would work with co-conspirators. As one Chicago player explained, the hustler might suggest to his victim that they play on a table near other players in on the scam who will subtly distract the mark and get a cut of the winnings once the games are over. Or, in 9-Ball, a player might not notice his opponent consistently placing the 1 and 9 balls on the outside of each rack. This gets the player used to seeing the balls distributed a certain way on a break, and once the player is in a groove, the balls will be racked differently, making for a different break spread and throwing off his game.

"Chicago is the third-largest city in the country. But why aren't there any tournament stops here?" one of my sources said. "You want to gamble, we want to rob."

Sandbagging is the APA's version of hustling, though gambling of any kind on its matches is, of course, disallowed by the organization; the only money that should be changing hands is the green fee paid to the bar every night. But this doesn't mean there aren't ways to make money playing in the APA. One could gamble under the table, and this does happen, and a variety of APA-sponsored events held throughout the year offer cash prizes. At the Las Vegas tournament, dozens of MiniMania tournaments seem to be happening no matter the time of day or night; these tournaments often have no more than sixteen players each and offer prizes from tens of dollars to a few hundred dollars.[1] In fact, there's an entire subset of World Pool Championships attendees who come only for the Minnies without paying any attention to the larger tournaments taking place nearby, just as there are people who come to take advantage of the unlicensed $10 to $20 games happening in the semi-hidden Westgate side rooms stocked with a table or three. Those familiar with Las Vegas could no doubt rustle up even higher-paying action elsewhere in the city, as there are pool rooms that cater to the most serious of gambling clientele.

Brian Hale of Kickin' Like Bruce said he used to gamble on pool to help pay his college tuition, and that today some of his teammates like to gamble in Las Vegas but not necessarily on pool. Eli Mancha of the Billiard Men said he's never hustled in the traditional sense of the word, but he doesn't mind stepping up and flexing when he needs to. Once, when he was in rural Illinois, he saw someone ruthlessly take a bunch of money from a "friend" over the course of a few games, just humiliating the person and laughing when he lost. Mancha felt bad for the guy and in turn squashed the one who beat him—though he acknowledged he didn't feel bad enough to donate his winnings to the guy he'd stood up for.

Adina Fried of the BB Cues and her fiancé Eddie May go to Las Vegas regularly enough that they have an annual budget for such excursions, including a few thousand dollars set aside for gambling. May once won a bunch of money playing pool in Vegas, "beating up weekend warriors and retail players" who were there for an APA tournament, only to lose it gambling

---

1. MiniMania tournaments are open to all current APA members with at least twenty scores in one format within the preceding two years, but there you don't need to qualify to play; you can just sign up. Every game you play, including those in the Minnies, affects your handicap, so players need to make sure they're not playing so much that their individual handicap rises and jeopardizes the team's balanced handicap.

with an APA referee and then make a spectacular comeback and walk away with $5,000 more than he'd come in with. May's temperament is such that it's hard for him to back down from a challenge, and he is at the top of the list of people willing to bet big whenever the occasion arises. He is another example of a player who bridges the gap between the competitive but friendly APA and a riskier version of the game full of hustlers and sharks, and I had the opportunity to see the cutthroat side of his game one evening at City Pool Hall.

Each year, the Chicago River is dyed green in honor of St. Patrick's Day, and the city is blanketed by another sea of green in the form of hundreds of thousands of barhopping people wearing shamrock beads and tiny leprechaun hats. The revelry spilled into City Pool Hall, which happened to be hosting a Scotch doubles 8-Ball tournament that would send a two-person team to the Scotch doubles tournament at the World Pool Championships. (Players on a Scotch doubles team switch after every shot, as opposed to a single person continuing to shoot until he or she misses). The tournament was open to anyone in the local APA regardless of the standing of a player's team in the current season. As such, it was almost like a who's who of the Central Chicago leagues, with special two-person teams convened for the occasion. The tournament cost $25 per person to enter, with all proceeds going to fund the winning team's trip to Vegas.

Eddie May was there with his teammate, a 7 like himself, who was always open to serious competition. One of May's primary teams was Hundreds over Hardware, which played in the APA's Masters league, a league for higher-level players, generally high 5s and above.[2] He was playing at a table near the front of the bar. The circumstances of the game were making him play a bit more defensively than he normally would. He was obviously a skilled player, but a few observers didn't think much of how he was shooting his game. As he would relate, he kept hearing such comments as "Man, these

---

2. The Masters league follows a unique format adapted to the skills of its members. Each match is a race-to-seven split between 8-Ball and 9-Ball. The person who wins the lag gets to choose who gets to break or which game to play first. If 8-Ball is played first, five games are played before switching over to 9-Ball, with each win earning the player a single point. Seven games of 9-Ball are played if that game is chosen first, though it's typically best to choose 8-Ball first. As a more measured and defensive game, there is less of a risk of a player completely being shut out than in 9-Ball—players of Masters caliber can run racks without ever giving their opponent a chance to shoot. The teams play up to three matches, but if the first two are won by the same team, the game is over.

May named the team Hundreds over Hardware, which is to say, money means more to them than trophies, though Fried joked that, this being the APA, "all there is is hardware."

guys fuckin' suck!" or "That's some pussy pool!" coming from somewhere over his increasingly tense shoulders.

Finally, after their unsolicited observations continued for at least ten minutes, the game was over. He spun around and faced them.

"All right, let's put some fuckin' money on it, then," he said, catching them off-guard. He'd play any of them right there, right now, for $500 a game. He didn't give a *fuck*. "There's an ATM right there. Get some money and let's do this."

The guys fumbled over their words and retreated back into the crowd.

About ten minutes later, May was shooting at a side table with his brother Jackson, a bartender at Surge and a member of numerous APA teams, including the Billiard Men. The brothers were gregarious and welcoming but also had the air of men you could call on if you needed something handled.

"Look, I'm reformed, my brother's reformed. We grew up in a violent way, and at a different time, I would've just broken the cue over their heads," Eddie said. "Now, I'm trying to [*imitates deep breathing exercise*] and just let it go."

His brother nodded in agreement. "I'm a giant—a gentle giant. They never expect me. But then all the sudden BAM! I come out of nowhere and I'm right next to them!"

The two looked up and saw the ringleader of the drunk dudes walking over to them. His name was Brian, he said, and he asked if May wanted to play for money.

"Absolutely," he said, before Brian even finished talking.

As the sociologist Ned Polsky put it, a "player who claims that just playing the game is interesting itself is regarded as something of a freak." Although money is a great motivator for higher-stakes pool—if not *the* primary motivator—there is a significant element of pride at play as well. Chicago has always been a rough 'n' tumble city full of tough jobs and political agitation and has a proud underdog identity as the Second City to New York. This historic chip on its shoulder factored into the way the city played pool.

Being good at pool was a way for many players to challenge the circumstances they were dealt, offering a path toward recognition in a society in which options for mobility are limited. Performance on the table was a direct reflection of personal worth, status among peers, and the respectability of a player's block or neighborhood. Plus, hustling was certainly more exciting than a normal job for those who could handle the vicissitudes of the gambling life.

Eddie May is from Lake Zurich, a suburb northwest of Chicago. He worked in bars for well over a decade and is not afraid of a tougher approach to the game. "I grew up watching old hustlers play," he said. "Back in the day you'd never see halls filled with recreational players on a Tuesday."

May, now in his mid-thirties, lived on the road for a few years in his early twenties as a traveling salesman for a construction company, always eager to find a game when he could; his avocation overlapped easily enough with the wild life he was leading for a while. "I was making, like, $100,000 a year as a twenty-three-year-old," he said. "Just think of how stupid you could be with that kind of money." He eventually left that job to live in Europe for a while with his cousin, burned through his savings, and then came back and used his charms and social skills to work as a bartender and salesman in Chicago. Eventually, he and Adina Fried found themselves playing at the same table with an overlapping group of friends at City Pool Hall. Over the course of the next few years they'd move in together, raise two dogs, and start Bottles and Bouquets, an event catering business that specialized in alcohol and flowers, their respective areas of expertise. The pair had recently been engaged but were reworking their wedding plans after it turned out that chartering a plane to Jamaica was much more expensive than they'd realized. Despite being a high-level player who has played in the APA for years, May had never been on a team that won a trip to Vegas, a reality that perhaps added a chip of its own to his shoulders.

Many players soften with age or feel less inclined to answer every table-side challenge, but that was not the case on St. Patrick's Day at City Pool Hall. Eddie and Jackson May promptly walked over to the drunk guy's group to negotiate the terms of the match. Brian the instigator nominated a friend of his, William, who wasn't nearly as belligerent but seemed willing enough to compete. William said he only had around $100 cash, and he and May agreed on $50 per game. Brian overheard this and put a stop to it immediately.

"No! I thought we said $500!"

William's eyebrows shot up.

May smiled. "Great," he said.

"Can we do Venmo?" Brian asked.

May laughed. What was he going to do, send them a request to pay him? It was cash only.

The drunk guys dug through their pockets for as much as they could scrape together, which turned out to be around $400. "That's fine," May said. "Let's do it," and he agreed to use a bar cue like his opponent.

"Why would you challenge a guy in a pool hall?" he asked me off to the side. "We're here playing pool. In a tournament."

William broke, and May realized that the guy could make some shots, but that was about it. Higher-level ball control and the crucial defensive strategy of the game—the safeties they were mocking earlier as "pussy pool"—weren't even part of his vocabulary. At one point, May even stepped in to explain to William that he didn't have to shoot his scratch from the opposite end of the table—he could put it down anywhere on the table. His opponent looked at him almost gratefully. May rolled his eyes.

William sank a few balls in a row but May easily took the match. Had William been an actual pool player instead of merely the best shooter among his friends, he might have started to worry, May said. But he won fair and square, and the drunk dudes knew enough to be honest in their dealings. Four hundred cold, hard dollars changed hands, a positive outcome of an undertaking that can sometimes go sideways, as a number of Chicago APA players told me.

One recounted being punched by drunk college kids who didn't like being taken for $5 a shot, another talked about the perils of gambling for cocaine when the money ran out, and others recalled being straight up robbed of their winnings in the parking lot or even before they left the bar. (Road players usually credit the Deep South with having the most violent and unpredictable halls.) One player said he had a cue broken over his head by a drunk friend who accused him of stealing from his pile of winnings. It turned out the waitress had taken the money, but he had to get eighteen stitches as a result of the misunderstanding and was still hurt that his friend turned on him in such a way, especially because, when he'd gamble, he'd make sure not to beat someone so badly that the opponent felt humiliated. "I ain't gonna beat on nobody," the player said, shaking his head. "If they want their money back so bad, I'd just give it to 'em."

The first game between Eddie May and the drunks thus concluded peacefully, and Brian suggested they play again for another $400, which May agreed could be paid through Venmo since he'd just taken all their cash. William didn't seem thrilled about being put in the position of being responsible for their money once again, but May put the next game in motion before anyone could back out, effortlessly pocketing another $400. May typed his details into Brian's phone and hit Send himself to make sure the transfer went through.

By this point, Brian recognized he'd cost his friends money and that being a dickhead was clearly a mistake. "That's just who I am. I love talking shit. I'll talk shit 'til the day I die!" he said, by way of a pseudo-apology. May challenged him to a game and they settled on $20, which was one of the most vindicating and pathetic aspects of the whole affair—Brian had no problem talking shit and making his friend play with other peoples' money, but when it came time for him to put *his* money where his mouth is, he offered up a measly 1/20th of what his friends lost in a single game.

Unsurprisingly, May wiped him out and Brian looked genuinely deflated.

"You down for one more?" May asked, barely suppressing a smirk.

"No, we've got to go."

But the earlier tension had cooled by this point, and everyone was able to laugh as the challenge wound down.

"People think it's cool to be halfway good at pool, and it is. But most people don't want to put in the hours to get really good," May said. "They're the best among their friends but when they go into a bar, they're just good enough to lose a bunch of money."

May was glad to be in the right place at the right time to take up this kind of challenge. While there is still money being gambled around tables today, and there are still some go-to spots in Chicago if you're looking for action, that's more of an individual initiative and not part of the broader subculture as it used to be. One old-school player said it was video games that were most detrimental to young people's interest in pool (and being social in general), and technology does have a little bit to do with the changing dynamics of the game.

In the old days, players would go out of their way not to be recognized, turning down interviews and photos in order to preserve the element of surprise. Today, I was told, if an out-of-towner shows up looking for action, a candid photo might appear within minutes on any number of internet pool forums so people can figure out the player's identity and capability. On this day, however, some drunk dudes simply got a little loose and could afford to throw money around, and May happened to be a good enough player to take them down.

There were plenty of people at that moment playing in City Pool Hall who would've had no problem winning a match against those guys, May told me, but it takes a lot for someone to be comfortable putting $800 of his own money on the table.

A pool player walked up to him just as he was saying this.

"That was real cool, man! Fuckin' dumbasses. I was about to throw down with them for $500 but you beat me to it!"

May shot me a look.

As Fast Eddie says in *The Color of Money*, "Money won is twice as sweet as money earned," and, flush with cash, Fast Eddie May bought a round of shots for everyone near the table and tipped the waitress $50. If the win is a hard-earned game in a tournament, that's a personal victory and you get to keep every penny of it, he said. But if it's a situation like this, where you pick up $820 in about fifteen minutes off of some goofballs, that's party money that should be shared.

"To drunk bros and winning $800!" May said when the drinks arrived. Everyone laughed and threw back their shot.

Tales of the walloping were making their way around the Chicago APA within the hour. May and his entourage ended up at Gold Star Bar later that evening, and everyone who heard about what happened came over to congratulate him. Everyone likes seeing a braggart put in his place, and it was cool to know that one of their comrades took up the challenge and delivered—even if his various APA teams didn't go on to make it to Las Vegas that year.

CHAPTER 8

Racking Them Responsibly

A More Positive Appraisal of Pool and Its Place in Society

> The commercialism, the emotional outpouring,
> and the civic pride of [sporting events] . . . have
> been central to Chicago life and identity [and]
> remain fundamental to our urban self-definition.
>
> —"Creation of Chicago Sports"

When Ross Schaefer decided to buy the Chicago Central APA league, Gregg Taylor, who was selling it, gave him a lot of helpful guidance about the nuts and bolts of being an operator.[1] Schaefer was confident enough to hit the ground running, but what he didn't fully appreciate was the magnitude of the APA's requirement to grow the league by a certain number of teams each year. In the case of Schaefer's new charge, the requirement was to grow the league by fifty teams within two years.

Schaefer had taken over what was known as a conditional franchise, the condition being that he fulfill the expansion requirement or face being forced to sell the league, which is why Taylor was trying to offload it himself—being an operator required too much sweat equity to maintain. Even in a city such as Chicago, growing the league by twenty-five teams a year was a tall order, especially because the league had actually *shrunk* in the preceding couple of years. Hardcore players could be counted on to return session after session,

---

1. Taylor says he's personally given out more than $1.1 million in prize money in his life but often runs tournaments for "coffee and cigarettes," motivated first and foremost by his love of the game. He admits that this approach doesn't necessarily work when trying to run a profitable business, which is why he lost interest in running an APA league and dealing with what he says is the organization's somewhat rigid corporate approach to the sport. "Me and the APA don't see eye to eye," he said. "I'm not an easy guy to work with, but at least I'll work with ya."

but league pool was often one of the first indulgences to be cut by casual players when their schedules demanded it. When a team disbanded or a player stopped showing up, it could be a major step backwards because Schaefer would not only have to grow the league by the required number of teams but also replace the players and teams that left. And no matter how the league was doing, he was still on the hook for his monthly loan payments to Taylor.

"Every time a team quit, I'd have a panic attack," Schaefer said. "I didn't sleep well for a while."

Sometimes the APA would be forgiving if he got close to the yearly target, but then it would require him to make up the difference the next year on top of the new teams he was required to recruit. The growth requirements tapered off as Schaefer ran the league and proved himself a profitable operator capable of expanding the league into new neighborhoods and host locations. Within five years he was able to pay Taylor back and raise the status of his league so there were no more quotas to reach; any further growth was left to his ambition.

Schaefer attributed part of the league's growth to the revamped scoring system, which changed from a single point for each match victory to the 1/2/3-point system currently in use. (Three points for a shutout, two points for a win, one point if the loser wins a certain number of games.) This both sped things up and made them a bit more dramatic, as the high points awarded for a shutout provided a significant advantage to the winning team. Especially helpful, however, was the opening of the Surge Billiards location in Albany Park, a neighborhood west of downtown full of restaurants and bars and tons of foot traffic. As soon as Schaefer heard a new pool room was opening, he made sure plans for league play were in place. "I was in here before it looked anything like this," he said, gesturing around the finished bar and underlit bottles one evening as players went about their games. "When this place opened, my league doubled in value. Instantly. The opening of a nice place like this meant more tables and more players right away."

The Surge in Albany Park is one of two Surge locations owned and operated by Wahib Merchant (the other is in Logan Square), who is shaping up to be Chicago's pool hall magnate. Like the league operators who've made their love of the game work for them professionally, Merchant has found his niche in providing countless players with a place to play.

Merchant is an "accidental entrepreneur" who previously ran Pressure Billiards & Cafe at 6318 North Clark Street in the Edgewater neighborhood. He grew up in Chicago and played pool in many of the old haunts but, having majored in IT work, he never imagined he would own a hall of his own. At one point, however, he noticed that activities in which people go out to do things—visiting arcades, ax throwing, bowling—seemed to be going through a resurgence. He saw an opportunity and took it upon himself to learn the complicated world of opening a business in Chicago. "I was a bit younger then, a bit less risk averse," he laughed.

Pressure Billiards helped him find his footing in the Chicago pool and business world and, a career in IT far behind him, he wanted his next endeavor to feel a little more sophisticated than the average pool room. The plan was to have the Surge Billiards locations serve as coffeeshops/pool halls during the day and cocktail bars/pool halls in the evening, with a classy aesthetic that serves this dual purpose. Merchant's crew started gutting the space in March 2017, announcing in *Eater Chicago* that the refurbished hall would feature "fourteen Brunswick Crown V pool tables, a 20-seat bar, and room for about 40 more seats inside a 6,000-square-foot space." The first Surge opened in 2018 and the second in 2020.

"The question I normally get is, 'You own a pool hall? How many fights do you see?' But this place really surprises people," Merchant said.

Surge is in a building previously known as the home of Marie's Golden Cue, a pool hall that was open for almost fifty years. The large sign out front notoriously read, "We have smooth shafts and clean balls." Once, a man called to tell co-owner Ted Minassian that he passed the sign driving his children to school and thought it was "despicable." "I just simply said to him 'Sir, we're a pool hall in case you haven't noticed,'" Minassian said. "'We do have smooth shafts and we clean balls, OK? I can't help where your mind's at,' and I hung up on him."

Minassian co-owned the place with his wife Norma, daughter of the eponymous Marie. In response to the requests that he put in a TV or a jukebox, he'd tell people to go watch the game somewhere else or go to a club to dance. "This is pure pool," he'd say. The indoor smoking ban of 2007 impacted his business—"pool and cigarettes are like peanut butter and jelly"—and he faced further problems with the 2008 recession. He finally put the hall up for sale when he was diagnosed with cancer in 2013, and that led to Merchant's picking it up.

Though Merchant specifically chose the location to keep the older pool room's history alive, he isn't as much of a purist. Music thumps throughout the night, TVs keep people updated on the latest in sports and news, movies from the '80s and '90s play in the background, and the "smooth shafts" sign is long gone. "It was like a marker of the community," said Billiard Men captain Eli Mancha. "I told him he should have kept it up."

The crudeness of the sign notwithstanding, pool halls have often played a positive role in their community, if those benefits went unnoticed in favor of the more sordid stories of drunks and gamblers. Even at the height of public skepticism about the social benefits of pool, there were plenty of adherents who argued that pool *itself* wasn't corrupt but, rather, the unfortunate surroundings in which it was played. In the nineteenth century, advocates for the sport used the momentum of the public's growing interest in sports to popularize the game, partnering with a variety of organizations and manufacturers to expand the game beyond the walls of the danker pool halls.

Chicago itself was also critical to the game's growth because the city was once home to sporting goods manufacturers such as Schwinn, Spalding, Brunswick, and Wilson, all of which took advantage of the city's strategic midwestern location and the economic boom that followed the Great Chicago Fire of 1871.[2] The concentration of skilled artisans in the city supplied a labor force capable of making incredibly ornate pool tables (and the matching bars and furniture to go with them) and came up with ways to streamline the process of manufacturing pool tables to keep up with demand.[3] These companies provided high-quality equipment that not only gave American tables a more noble bearing but created the standardized sizes that for the most part have remained unchanged since then.

Chicago-made tables and equipment spread throughout the country while manufacturers partnered with local pool halls to sponsor tournaments that made celebrities of the best shooters. Manufacturers also worked with civic groups such as the Catholic Youth Organization to sponsor athletics programs and provide tables and equipment to community centers. These organizations were woven into the social and civic fabric of the day, and, in addition to giving neighborhood kids something productive to do, were known for incubating top-notch players.

Over time, Brunswick emerged as the leader of its cohort and used its cachet to help out the Chicago Bowling and Billiards Protective League, which was convened in 1915 to promote the sport and continue to clean up its reputation. Chicago's pool halls knew their reputations would benefit from

---

2. The fire incinerated almost eighteen thousand buildings and claimed among its victims local billiard hotshot John McDevitt, whose "velvet touch" helped him beat an opponent so badly that certain techniques were banned from tournaments from that point on.

3. According to one advertorial, the Brunswick factory provided three hundred workers with "fair wages which are promptly paid," and by giving each worker his own tools, table, and window, contact between people was minimized and "thus quarrels are prevented." However, Brunswick's employees went on strike in 1885 after twenty years of petitioning for better working conditions. As Chicago sports scholar Gerald Gems writes, Brunswick's workers "suffered the humiliation of having to return to the workplace and reclaim their own tools from the hands of scab labourers."

the league's stamp of approval because, in order to obtain it, each hall owner had to "conduct his bowling alley or billiard hall in an orderly and unobjectionable manner" that discouraged illegal practices. But the league also stuck up for the sport, endorsing local candidates amenable to the interests of the billiard world and providing league-retained counsel for hall owners accused of promoting gambling. After all, it was hard to separate the two: At one hall, a sign on the walls read, "No gambling allowed," while the floor manager was loudly calling for bets.

Powerful businesses such as the Pullman Company put clubhouses with pool tables in their company town south of Chicago, though one needn't be overly cynical to guess at the motivation for doing so. As Chicago architectural historian John Cramer writes, whereas people once feared that playing pool would make people unproductive, here companies provided pool rooms to "distract the resentful worker with an unending schedule of events, and exhaust the younger, more energetic . . . workers through company-sponsored sports leagues. Under the watchful eye of his employer, the worker's mind could be kept firmly on making money for the parent company, and not be allowed to wander to foolish and dangerous anarchical notions."

Whether a game with a dubious past, a pacifying distraction, or simply a challenging game of precision, pool was so widely played by the dawn of the twentieth century that it supported a mini-economy that provided a livelihood for a variety of industries and professions, from equipment manufacturers to newspaper publishers to league operators and bar owners, and a version of that economy was sustained in Chicago by places like Marie's and its peers Bensinger's and Chris's, with many more classic dives and the local shooters competing in the tournaments they hosted now consigned to history. On a broader scale, the earnings possible in this industry no doubt helped improve the game's reputation further, especially during the waves of pool's popularity.

Besides, it wouldn't be pool players whose in-game antics let down an entire nation—that distinction was reserved for the wholesome enterprise that was baseball. In 1919, a few players on the Chicago White Sox conspired with bookies to throw the World Series against the Cincinnati Reds. The revelation that it was the players themselves who had orchestrated the cheating was so shocking and so distressing that it "may have been more important than World War I in educating the nation in the dubious lessons of disenchantment." Those involved were considered the "ultimate scum of the universe," "betrayers of American Boyhood, not to mention American Girlhood and American Womanhood and American Hoodhood." Such an offense made gambling on pool seem like a quaint if not obscure hobby, or at least made people more pragmatic about the fact that any game could be seized on for unethical ends. Indeed, scandals have popped up in practically every sport since then, proving that human nature is to blame and not the nature of a specific game.

In present-day Chicago, Wahib Merchant is a firm believer in the potential of pool and the pool community. Surge's website and publicity materials don't refer to the place as a pool hall, as he pointed out. Surge is a social hub above all, a part of the neighborhood, and he's used the locations to host corporate parties, political events, and fundraisers of all kinds.[4] These are just the beginnings of what a pool hall can offer, he said, and he's already planning for a third Surge location to expand these offerings further. An APA league will no doubt be in place by the time the doors are ready to open, providing the crucial component that keeps halls solvent: dedicated players.

"Believe it or not, [I'm] not sick of pool yet," Merchant laughed. The sound of clacking balls and conversation and music thrumming in the background of a pool hall is a comforting ambiance to those who love the game, no matter what difficulties running such an establishment might inspire.

"It relieves stress," he said. "It's just you and the balls. It's kind of peaceful actually."

---

4. According to the website, "Surge aims to be a place where the diversity of the area is represented in the diversity of the services we offer. Come work, shoot pool, have drinks with friends or sip coffee . . . just know you're welcome!"

CHAPTER 9

As the Cue Ball Turns

Criminals, Pool Halls, and Drama in the APA

"As the Cue Ball Turns"—that's what I call pool drama.

—Gregg Taylor

Although the images of mobsters, crime, and pool are deeply intertwined, as far as I could tell, the pool trade in Chicago has never specifically been under the control of a criminal organization. This isn't to say that gangsters didn't own pool halls in order to launder money through them, that criminals didn't take their percentages from neighborhood joints, or that gangs didn't put up money to back pool players in high-stakes games. All of this definitely happened—the Chicago mob, known as the Outfit, was hugely powerful and certainly had its hands in all kinds of schemes and investments (including a legendarily corrupt justice system). Al Capone reportedly owned a pool hall or two, as did South Side gangster William "Flukey" Stokes, who was well-known for burying his son in a Cadillac with hundred-dollar bills sticking out from between his fingers. Unfortunately, I did not get to interview many mobsters for this book and thus wasn't able conduct a full survey of the overlap of pool and the criminal profession in Chicago.[1] Still, it wasn't difficult to find crime stories involving pool, from a Chicago mayor allegedly

---

1. A player from the Pilsen neighborhood gave some context about doing business in an area with a significant gang presence. The owner of his local hall had to get approval for the opening of the club from the heads of local gangs and had to get permission to have league play there. As long as everyone who comes to play is "cool," he said, and respects the area and doesn't cause trouble, the gangs have no problem with a pool hall. More people coming to the bars the gang owns, has a stake in, or collects protection money from means more money coming back to them. Plus, he added, it was a good way to keep tabs on who was coming into the area and why.

wanting to close pool halls because his son had been beaten up in one to a still-unsolved missing persons case.[2]

One of the crazier such stories took place in Chicago in the 1920s and involved Sam Cardinella, the "scariest gangster you never heard of." Cardinella ran a pool hall and was described as having some sort of "satanic" presence about him, a Fagan-like character and "human spider" who used his hall to turn wayward youth into violent criminals. Nicholas Vianna, the gang's eighteen-year-old second-in-command, was said to have committed his first murder within a week of entering the pool hall on his way home from choir practice. The gang managed to evade detection until a few members were captured at about the same time, with police determining that the gang had committed more than four hundred hold-ups and more than twenty murders within the preceding sixth months.

Vianna was ultimately executed for his many crimes (cursing Cardinella as he was about to die), and Cardinella himself was sentenced to death by hanging in April 1921. Though he bought himself some time—an hour, perhaps—when he petitioned his jailers to follow the schedule of the newly

2. Some choice cases: In November 1996, after getting beaten up in a fight with his long-time friend, Giovanni Spiller decided to get revenge. He ran up and shot the man in the head right in front of Marie's Golden Cue (which is now Surge Billiards), killing him. Spiller eventually fled to the Philippines and avoided extradition thanks to issues caused by excess red tape. Years later a friend of Spiller's saw a story about the crime in the *Chicago Tribune* and didn't realize the severity of what he'd done, but he did know where Spiller was living—southern California—leading to his arrest and eventual sentence of thirty-five years behind bars.

An enduring mystery is the death of acclaimed player Michael "Biloxi Mike" Surber, who was found murdered in his home in Ocean Springs, Mississippi, in November 2009. According to the FBI, he was playing pool at a hall in Gulfport earlier the same day and was seen on security cameras shooting with a guy who looked like a movie hitman. Investigators learned that the pair made a handful of stops after leaving the pool hall together, including picking up a second vehicle of Surber's and taking it to his home. The next morning, Surber was found stabbed to death and his house robbed. The man on the video called himself "Jericho Cooper," as that was the name on the stolen credit card he was using, and it turned out he was seen on video at two additional pool halls around the time of Surber's murder. There has been no news of arrests or movement in the case beyond the initial investigation, but the case continues to be discussed in online true crime forums and pool message boards.

Pool hall owners could be some real tough cases, as well. Ramon Simpas Subejano, originally from the Philippines, traveled the world as a seaman and eventually came to the United States as a stowaway in a freighter. He bought a pool hall in Brooklyn, New York, with the $32,000 he made one night by gambling. His business was wiped out in the Great Depression but he became one of the most fearsome American soldiers of World War II, single-handedly killing more than four hundred Nazis and earning medals from at least four countries.

instituted Daylight Savings Time, he was led to the gallows all the same, noticeably thinner from a sustained hunger strike. Cardinella reportedly lost his composure completely as he got closer, collapsing and freaking out to the degree that he had to be tied to a chair and dropped from the rope while sitting down. The executioner went through with the deed, and Cardinella was carted off in a waiting ambulance instead of a hearse. Thinking this was odd, authorities stopped the ambulance and whipped open the doors to find a team of doctors and nurses trying to bring Cardinella back to life.

It turned out that Cardinella's freakout was a ruse to get him tied to a chair so that he'd have a shorter drop on the rope; the fall also was eased, in theory, because of the weight he'd lost. They'd earlier tried the same thing successfully on Vianna, allegedly reviving him after he was only strangled instead of having his neck broken, but Vianna was supposedly *killed again* as punishment for talking to authorities about the gang's exploits. Cardinella's plan was only partly successful—he'd avoided breaking his neck when he dropped—but he was strangled to death by the rope all the same, and no amount of emergency care could bring him back to life.

Fortunately, most of the issues that today's pool hall owners must deal with are a little less deadly, if not still fairly heated, including the occasional beef with APA league operators.

An hour northwest of Chicago in a suburb called Algonquin is an unassuming pool hall called the Twisted Rose, which sits on a developed yet tree-lined corner where a state route intersects with a highway. The place has around a dozen seven-foot tables and is known for hosting some of Chicagoland's highest-paying tournaments, which means a lot of the people in the Chicago leagues are surprisingly familiar with an otherwise obscure suburban hall. It also boasts remarkably good home-cooked Polish food made by owner Teresa Wesolowski that is so delicious that it helped the place stay open during the pandemic—people were happy to come and wait in their cars to get some of her amazing cooking, which in turn prompted a successful side catering business.

The Twisted Rose is overseen in part by Freddie Norris, who is Wesolowski's on-again, off-again partner. A thin, middle-aged man in a crewneck sweatshirt who looks as if he could be in a 1980s movie, he grew up playing with shooters who were quite serious about their reputations. "It would be, like, 'Hey, Joe Blow from North or South Naperville is calling you out,'" he said. "Or, 'There's a party this weekend and there's a pool table. Bring some money.'"

In addition to running tournaments and helping out at the bar, Norris also helped coordinate league play at the Twisted Rose, which has historically been home to the mid-sized Fox Valley APA league. The bar has a wall full of APA plaques attesting to victories in 8-Ball and 9-Ball tournaments dating back years, and astute observers may note that the official names on the plaques switch from APA to BCS starting around the fall of 2018.

According to sources in the Twisted Rose's corner, the loss of the Fox Valley APA league allegedly started with the strongarm tactics of the franchise's former owner, whom I'll refer to as Josh. Josh was said to withhold the nightly table fees from the Twisted Rose, discourage people from eating there or playing the gambling machines, and, when accused of doing this, threaten to stop bringing people to the bar. The league players who called him out were said to have their handicaps adjusted disadvantageously or threatened with expulsion if they played one of the other leagues at the Twisted Rose. "You're nothing without the APA," Josh was said to have told the establishment's owners, and he allegedly even started a rumor that he was going to report the bar to the Health Department for selling glasses of water, which Norris said they were not doing. The accusations and counter-recriminations led to bad blood all around, forcing many league players and bar patrons to choose sides. (All this at a place that received the 2019 McHenry County Best Billiard Establishment Award, no less.)

"I saw [the owner] in the grocery store and walked up and said, 'Why do you tell so many lies?'" Norris said. "Then I turned to the cashier and said, 'This man's a liar!' and I walked out. His hands were shaking so bad." A similar encounter reportedly took place at a gas station as well.

Eventually Norris wrote what he happily referred to as a "manifesto" to the APA that outlined the issues he had with the franchise owner. The hope was that the dossier would make such a compelling case that the APA would have no choice but to strip the owner of his right to operate the league. It was a point of pride for Norris and the Twisted Rose that they wouldn't be bullied into putting up with this behavior just so that they could host the league.

"BEWARE ALL APA PLAYERS AND ALL APA BAR HOST LOCATIONS (HL), THIS COULD HAPPEN TO YOU," the letter began.

However, Walter Burkart III, APA's director of franchise operations, was not particularly receptive to these complaints.

"Many, in fact most of the points you listed below are inaccurate, incomplete, rumors or just lack the context required to give the statement adequate perspective," he wrote in his response. "I will simply state that while you disagree with the [franchise owner's] reasoning and consistently attack his character and business, he has the right not to do business with any host location."

The APA would not force the owner to sell the franchise, nor would it force Josh to conduct APA business at an establishment with which he had a problem. "You'll excuse me for being direct," Burkhart wrote, but he just wanted to be crystal clear about his thoughts.

The issue eventually worked itself out when Josh's personal problems deprioritized running a pool league and he dropped out of sight. It's unclear where he ended up, but rumor has it he left the Midwest completely. Soon thereafter, the new owners stepped in to try to pick up the pieces of the Fox Valley league.

Mark Covalt was always a fan of the sport, having grown up shooting around with his brothers. As a serial entrepreneur who has worked in everything from selling vacuums to investing in real estate, his ears perked up when he learned that running a pool league was a viable way to earn a living. He and Joy, his wife and business partner, couldn't find any franchises interested in selling, but one day Mark was playing in a tournament at the Twisted Rose and got to talking to Josh, who by this point was trying to offload his ownership of the league. "You'll never believe what's going on," Mark said to Joy, and within two weeks an agreement to take over the league was in place.

The league regrew steadily in the first six months as people were eager to get back to playing in a more stable environment, but Covalt soon found that the long-term players had a reflexive resistance to any ideas or changes he suggested. There was still bad blood from the former owner's spat with the Twisted Rose, and Mark had players yell in his face and call him names, all over fairly minor disagreements, with some of this behavior being in solidarity with the former owner. Josh apparently had problems with other area bars as well, broadening the enmity toward the APA and limiting the available places for league play. Soon Covalt saw the number of teams in his league drop by almost 40 percent. He said his usual reaction, as someone who was bullied growing up, used to be to get right back in people's face when they got in his, but he knew as a business owner there was a better way to handle it, and he and Joy sat down to figure out ways to improve morale. Excessively negative and troublesome players were pruned from the roster, the olive branch of new league ownership was extended to area bars, and overall attitudes finally became more relaxed as people saw the couple were sincere in their regard for the league.

Since then, the Fox Valley APA has seen a steady increase in the number of its teams. The couple trained their son to be the league's office manager, freeing time up for Mark to continue building the league, continue scouting and putting together teams, and glad-hand players and bar owners.

"With the APA, they've got a system that works," he noted. "If you work the system, it will run your business. As an entrepreneur, I love systems, I know they're key to running a business."

The earning and employment potential of healthy league play is, in part, why APA founders Terry Bell and Larry Hubbart were inducted into the Billiard Congress of America's Billiard Hall of Fame in 2010. The pair were recognized for their meritorious service to the game of pool by bringing so many players to the game, a population and interest that in turn support the livelihoods of people like the Covalts, Teresa Wesolowski, Ross Schaefer, and Wahib Merchant.

"Honestly, I struggle to look at any other entity that's had a greater impact on the sport," said APA national marketing director Jason Bowman. "The APA has had well over a million members throughout our history, and these players are buying every imaginable piece of pool equipment, going to every hall, putting pool tables in their homes. If you took APA out of the picture, I have no idea what pool would look like."

But there's another reason why hall owners, league operators, and APA employees are grateful to have found a way to make the business of pool their livelihood. As invincible as you might feel when you rule over a table, the grind to make it as a professional player can be just as challenging as the struggles of a down-and-out hustler.

CHAPTER 10

A Real Hustle

The Difficult Pathway to the Pros

City Pool Hall owner Cathy Nitti went about her task of looking over the books in a small cinderblock office that shares a wall with an alcove that contains a Deer Hunter arcade machine. Although she runs the place, she doesn't have the enthusiasm for the sport that her brother, who originally opened the hall, did. She took over as owner after he died and said she just looks at it like a business before pushing the door closed with her foot.

Behind the bar, Krystal Glenn looked over at her nephew Michael. She used to take him and the other nieces and nephews who worked at City Pool Hall to play in the park when they were kids, but now young Michael was stepping up in the family business. He followed a flustered new member out of the kitchen into the bar. "It's not sit-down time when you're done in the kitchen!" he scolded. "Come out here and see what you can do." Glenn smiled with pride.

She was also proud of the more-vibrant-than-normal table felt, which was newly installed. City Pool re-felts its tables approximately once per year and had recently done so in anticipation of an upcoming tournament.

The re-felting process was a serious undertaking that required the hall to close for at least three days. The tables have to be disassembled, the felt evenly stretched, and everything put back together so the playing surface is perfectly level and the felt—a wool or a wool-nylon blend—is evenly stretched without any runs that could throw a ball off course.

"They said it would take 100 to 150 games to break the new felt in," Glenn said. "I said, 'Great, it'll be ready by tonight or tomorrow.'"

One of the people responsible for breaking in the new felt was league player Milo Dalton,[1] an attorney who is so good that he was raised to a 7 on

---

1. A pseudonym.

his first night in the APA despite never having played in the league before. Both Ross Schaefer and Gregg Taylor said Dalton was hands down the best player they've ever had in the league, a person whose natural talent for the game is almost chosen-one prophetic.

One evening at City Pool Hall, Dalton, who was playing a fellow attorney, told me he'd never taken lessons or had a coach; he just watched and learned and internalized every single aspect of the game. His technique just seemed to come together perfectly, from the way his tall, lanky figure stretched over the table to the way he was able to calculate and execute practically any shot no matter the angle or the balls standing in the way. His game was captivating, smooth and effortless and as close to genuine pool poetry as I've ever seen.

Dalton won numerous regional tournaments when he was in college, as the odd jobs he was doing afforded him the time he needed to practice and play extensively. Pool was put on hold as he went through law school, and he extended the pause further when he took a job as a personal injury lawyer. Once he settled into his groove as an attorney, he realized how much he missed playing pool and began going to bars in Ukrainian Village looking for a game. A friend of a friend knew Ross Schaefer, and Dalton soon found himself on a team. "I try to go out there and have fun," he said. "I'm not as competitive as I once was."

Unfortunately, the ability to have fun took a hit when his team, the Ramen Boys, was accused of sandbagging by their opponent SECS at citywides, leading to a series of onsite conversations and arguments that in turn led to the APA's being called in to arbitrate. Dalton himself wasn't accused of sandbagging—there's no way he could disguise his talent—but was considered possibly part of a team-wide plot to help others do it. Having his reputation besmirched was not an experience that made him keen to keep playing in the APA, and he knew that he was good enough to play at the highest levels of competition if he wanted to. The bigger the risk, the bigger the reward, and he was a player capable of taking some seriously big risks.

Once a player gets good enough, the first step out of local league play might be to compete in the various county, state, or regional tournaments held throughout the year. These tournaments offer cash prizes, and the bigger tournaments tend to attract the area's best players (including many of the higher-level players in Chicago's APA leagues) as well as professionals if the prize pot is large enough. Tournaments like these help players get a sense of the current landscape of competition and what they need to do to advance their professional ambitions.

But in order to understand this trajectory, it's important to clarify what being a professional pool player means.

There are a variety of official-sounding organizations that claim to be the most official body for pool, and one, the World Pool-Billiard Association, has regional affiliates in every continent with a set of standardized rules that are used across many major tournaments.[2] But there is no NBA-style professional pool league that drafts players. Instead, there are a number of organizations and sponsors that host the tournaments that make up a de facto professional circuit, and pro players make the rounds of these events.[3] Perennial favorites such as Indiana's Derby City Classic always bring in top players, and pool equipment companies such as Predator host their own serious affairs. Matchroom Sport, a UK-based company that had some luck popularizing televised darts, hosts live-streamed pool tournaments that pay out tens of thousands of dollars to the top finishers. These tournaments include the Mosconi Cup, an event alternately held in England and the United States that is named after legendary player Willie Mosconi and is essentially the sport's most prestigious tournament.

Players are ranked across these tournaments by the Fargo rating system, which is an ongoing ranking affected by one's performance in any sanctioned event, à la chess's FIDE system or the APA's Equalizer. The top players in the world have Fargo ratings in the low-to-mid 800s, and the best players in the Chicago APA leagues are probably in the 600s.

Given the time needed to practice, travel, and compete, most aspiring and recognized professionals can't hold full-time jobs. Some top-level players have backers who help fund their expenses (and day-to-day lives, if they want them to practice more than work), and these players in turn owe their backers a cut of their earnings. Perhaps the overall highest-paying tournament ever was in 1859, when the "father of American pool," Michael Phelan, beat John Seereiter for the equivalent of $400,000; the highest-paying pool tournaments today typically award top prizes of tens of thousands of dollars at most. If you don't place highly (or at all, because there are dozens of excellent competitors vying for the same prizes) you might not even make back the cost of getting to the tournament in the first place.

All told, the top five professionals in the world today—not the top 5 percent, the top *five*—might make over $100,000 per year playing pool, with the

---

2. The WPA represents pool in the World Confederation of Billiards Sports, which in turn represents all forms of cue sports (including carom billiards and snooker) on the International Olympic Committee. The APA has positioned itself as the governing body of amateur pool, comparing the organization in a newspaper ad to the United States Golf Association when a USGA event was being hosted in St. Louis.

3. The APA says of itself that the organization is "generally recognized as the Governing Body of Amateur Pool, having established the official rules, championships, formats and handicap systems for the sport of amateur billiards."

top three generally breaking $150,000. Shane Van Boening, the best player in the United States and ranked number 6 globally, had earned approximately $66,000 for the year as of July 2023, with about $2.2 million in earnings over the course of his nearly twenty-year professional career. Most players not in the top fifteen struggle to take in more than $40,000 annually from the sport.

Of course, top pros get perks such as cues, accessories, and even tables from their sponsors, and well-known players can give clinics or individual lessons that can cost hundreds of dollars per person per session. Many open their own pool halls, while others look for interesting investment opportunities, such as a sports-oriented energy drink called Extreme Focus. One of the most successful players in terms of sponsorships is Jeanette "Black Widow" Lee, whose sponsors have included Rocawear, Bass Pro Shops, and online betting websites, and some of today's top professionals are said to have sponsorship deals that add up to a few hundred thousand dollars per year. Social media can be another source of pool-related income if you know how to monetize it.

To be sure, pool is a fairly niche sport that's never going to have the mass appeal of baseball or UFC, but many pool enthusiasts feel the game's potential has been hindered by the lack of a definitive professional league and the organization and resources it could put into marketing the sport.

Although mainstream networks occasionally show pool programming or broadcast major tournaments, the lack of a successful professional league means there has never been a large enough fan base to sustain a dedicated pool network. In the modern era, pool-specific streaming services and online communities have stepped in to pick up the slack. Samsung TV now has Billiard TV, while streaming services like DAZN and various pool channels on YouTube are some of the most prominent places to go for broadcast pool, including major events such as the Mosconi Cup. This exposure has helped bring the sport to newer and younger audiences, many of whom are coming into the sport with astonishing proficiency thanks to the endless pool content available on the internet.

This isn't to say that there haven't been attempts to get professional leagues going. The Professional Cuesports Association was a "renegade tour group" started by Texas pool pro C. J. Wiley that launched with an eight-person pro tournament in 1996. The league made headlines when its founders announced that it would pay out a million dollars to anyone who could run ten racks consecutively during the tournament. Famously temperamental 9-Ball shooter Earl "The Pearl" Strickland ran ten racks on the tournament's first day, an accomplishment so unexpected, and the PCA so new, that the league's insurance company refused to pay the promised million-dollar prize.

A series of lawsuits filed in pursuit of the money bankrupted the fledgling league.[4]

Another was the International Pool Tour, which at one point did offer some of the largest prize pools in the history of the sport, including lucrative fees paid to pros for playing exhibition matches. Founded by billionaire infomercial mogul Kevin Trudeau, the IPT was modeled on the classic pool era, with tournaments held in elegant casino ballrooms and players required to wear suits.

The inaugural event was the 2005 IPT North American Open, which drew more than two hundred participants from forty countries and was streamed live for a week in Europe. Efren Reyes, a low-key Filipino player who is considered the greatest pool player of all time, won $200,000, and players were guaranteed amounts for exhibition matches that would be beyond first prize money in other tournaments. The following year, however, organizers claimed that the checks weren't on site and that players would instead be paid a few weeks later. It turned out that the IPT had run into major financial problems and ultimately took more than a year and nine separate installments to pay players back. One pro said his nerves were so shot by the affair that it affected his performance for the entire year.

Trudeau noted in one of his communiqués to the players that it was "legally unacceptable" for him, a billionaire, to front the prize money himself, but it turned out Trudeau was doing more than making up excuses—he was a straight up con artist. He'd been imprisoned for credit card fraud, was accused by the Illinois Attorney General of running a pyramid scheme, and was under investigation by numerous state and federal agencies for the products his companies sold, including a weight loss program that involved not exercise but a regimen of humming and light taps to the body and face. He was fined hundreds of thousands of dollars on numerous occasions and was forever banned from "appearing in, producing, or disseminating future infomercials that advertise any type of product, service, or program to the public."

Eventually, the IPT stopped hosting major tournaments and focused instead on live-streaming well-paying matches between pro players, but this endeavor petered out as well, bringing the IPT brand to a close. Not only was the loss of potential disappointing to pool players, but Jon Wertheim, former editor of *Sports Illustrated*, went as far as to say that the IPT was

---

4. The use of only ten racks seems to be poorly thought out. Willie Mosconi sank 526 balls in one stretch playing straight pool in 1954 (balls are continuously re-racked in straight pool), but this record was crushed in 2019 when pro shooter John Schmidt sank 626 balls in a row.

the "final squirt of embalming fluid" that "killed" the classic pool hustling culture. According to Wertheim, the chance to compete for six or even seven figures was simply too good an opportunity to pass up and brought out of the shadows many of the hustlers who otherwise preferred to remain anonymous. When the IPT didn't turn into a sustainable pro league, hustlers were too exposed and couldn't go back to their previous tricks. "While there are, admittedly, figures more deserving of sympathy than unemployed pool players, the demise of the hustler is an occasion to be mourned," Wertheim wrote. "The death of hustling marks the end of a uniquely American pursuit."

The game's historical association with gambling is the reason why some players believe pool or billiards has never been featured in the Olympics, though others argue that pool is simply more a game than a sport and thus shouldn't be included. The World Pool-Billiard Association essentially serves as the international governing body for the sport, but there isn't a global pool infrastructure robust enough to organize tournaments that consistently conform to an Olympic standard. It's also possible that the game just isn't popular enough to warrant inclusion. Fans, players, and organizations continue to lobby the International Olympic Committee to include pool, but there doesn't seem to be any positive movement in that direction. If this changes, or if there is another billionaire willing to start a pro league, more people would almost certainly be drawn to the sport, though there will always be the hundreds of thousands of players perfectly content with their weekly (or nightly) league matches and who will play regardless of what's happening outside their local halls.

Chicago APA players such as Milo Dalton, who are good enough to play professionally, appreciate the opportunity the league offers to stay sharp, and they recognize the de facto mentorship role they have stepped into as some of the best in the league. The chance to learn from someone of that caliber is an experience not every team can provide, and players are eager to soak up all the insight they can.[5]

---

5. Jeff Gussman, one of the top players in the Chicago APA, is typically surrounded by an entourage eager to learn something from his capacity to win. Like his twin brother, Gussman is also an accomplished poker player, and he played a poker app on his phone between shots, coolly glancing at his two cards and then back at the table. He was the captain of a team that placed fifth at the world championships, one of the first times a team from the area achieved a high ranking in recent memory, and the win netted the team approximately $5,000. Gussman's share was enough pocket money to turn into some serious scratch when he hit the tables. Indeed, even if the team took first place and he got his share of the $25,000 prize, he said, "That's really not that much money. I could make more than that playing poker in a weekend."

But the visibility of high-caliber players also means league operators hold them to a higher standard, almost as if they are ambassadors for the APA. Perceived contravention of this duty is taken very seriously, which is why it seemed particularly tragic when Milo Dalton got caught up in the sandbagging allegations lobbed at his team the Ramen Boys at the 2022 citywides, like the smart kid in school caught doing something bad. Whether or not the allegations were true was the subject of fierce debate.

According to some players who, once again, preferred to remain anonymous, scrutiny of Chicago's high-level players wasn't without precedent. There were rumors that in the 1980s and '90s a number of Chicago's best shooters joined the APA not because of an interest in growing the league but because they knew they could easily win the prize money and free trip, which they did and tried to do again until they were banned. Perhaps word of Chicago's reputation at the APA made its way back to league operators such as Ross Schaefer, who were extra sensitive in the interest of keeping his league clean and fair. (I did broach this topic here and there over the course of working on this book to some of the people mentioned as gaming the APA system, but such accusations were obviously denied.)

The APA's eventual ruling on the Ramen Boys–SECS sandbagging allegation included adjusting players' handicaps in such a way that it upset the balance of the team so that the highest-ranked players, including Dalton, wouldn't be able to continue playing. And that's why Dalton found himself in the strange position of simultaneously being the best player in the Chicago Central APA and disqualified from playing in Las Vegas, a Lebron James–like figure who could single-handedly carry the team, if not the tournament.

The Ramen Boys steadfastly maintained that they were playing the game straight, and the allegations and counter-allegations meant that matters became heated and personal. Each side felt that the other had said unkind words and even issued vague threats, and Dalton left voluntarily before he could be asked to leave.

"If it was fair, it wouldn't be the APA," I heard one player grumble.

The Ramen Boys ultimately did make it to Vegas that year, but the scrutiny was intense. One of the teammates said she felt as if the APA was watching them almost as soon as they arrived, much more intensely than she was expecting even knowing they were on thin ice. She said league officials were short with her when she went to retrieve some of the team's paperwork, and then acted like conspiring detectives whispering about her and the team from behind the officials' tables. She looked genuinely rattled after recounting to me how much suspicion was directed toward them.

Sometimes teams will be able to plead their case to a tribunal of officials, but the Ramen Boys didn't get this chance at vindication because they were disqualified when their ever-changing handicap situation precluded them from moving any further in the tournament. The APA's extremely careful scrutiny of their score sheets revealed enough inconsistencies for the organization to make this determination in good faith, although there wasn't enough direct evidence they'd purposefully sandbagged.

The punishment a team is given depends on the severity of the accusations and the patterns the data reveal. It is intended to be strict enough to dissuade teams from sullying the APA's reputation. Fortunately, it didn't come to any sort of ban for the Ramen Boys, for it was still plausible that the handicapping saga was more the result of sloppy bookkeeping than malicious cheating. But the whole situation cast a pall over the team's next few seasons, and Milo Dalton never returned to play in the Chicago APA. He's since started a law firm that has drawn accolades from his attorney peers, which means it's unlikely he'll forgo his legal career to try his luck at professional pool. But if he ever did, it might not be long before he became one of the lucky souls who could earn a living playing the game—and without any whispers of resorting to shady tactics to make it happen.

CHAPTER 11

The Organizer and the Inventor

Two Dedicated Players Try to Forge a Path Beyond the Table

Given the unique stressors and unconventional hours of running a pool league (not to mention the occasional hard-hitting sandbagging accusation), Ross Schaefer acknowledged he occasionally feels a bit burnt out by pool and almost welcomed the required pause in league play as the COVID pandemic got into full swing.

Over the course of the shutdown, Schaefer left a ten-year relationship, recorded and released an album, and thought about getting a band together and going back to being a full-time musician. But, he realized, "It's got to be a good offer if I'm going to start a new life and career," and none of the musicians he'd intermittently jammed with seemed reliable enough to make this happen. But the most impactful idea was "going with the flow" and relocating to parts unknown with a nomadic new woman he was seeing, perhaps picking up pool again in a different locale or moving on to a new pursuit altogether.

Unfortunately, the invitation to accompany her on her travels wasn't extended, and her hitting the road without him hit Schafer harder than he expected. The thought of running the league again, as stressful as it could be, seemed like a welcome distraction, and he was ready to get back to it in the spring of 2021, when the post-COVID APA started pressuring him to get things going again.

Despite the headaches, Schaefer is certainly happy to operate a league for a living and did try to constantly remind himself how good he has it, and even when he was telling me about something stressful, he always made sure to point out he loved what he was doing. But, he told me, if he wanted to meet someone who was wildly enthusiastic about even the most bureaucratic aspects of managing a league, there was one guy in particular he needed to talk to. Aside from the league operators, nobody else he talked to expressed an interest in running a league, let alone aspired to do so, but these ambitions reflect why some players want to do more than just play the game.

I asked Renee Glenn to point out Reggie Julun when I went to meet him at City Pool Hall one evening. "Oh, Reggie's crazy," she said, shaking her head and gesturing toward a tall man playing at a table in a back corner. This was coming from someone who spent a great deal of her time surrounded by crazy pool players, but it was true. While some people play on four or five teams at a time, Julun had recently been playing on *ten*. Sometimes he played on at least two teams each night, meaning he'd show up and shoot at one hall before taking the train or bus across town to play on another team.

"Well, I did downgrade to eight teams right now," Julun said when I went over to talk to him. "And I stopped being captain on five of them."

He was immaculately dressed in pressed pants, polished shoes, and a maroon shirt with a black tie, an ensemble that stood out in the casual hall. He explained that he'd once spent some time at the state capital in Springfield as part of a student government organization and took to heart the reality that people are often treated better when they look sharp. Despite being tall and strong, he spoke hesitantly and modestly at first, and said he made a point of looking extra nice because he knew a writer was coming to talk to him.

He started playing pool relatively late in life but quickly took to the sport because of his tendency to dive headfirst into whatever he's interested in.

"I was a family man from about 22 to 28, living with my girlfriend and her three kids," he said. "We broke up in 2014 and I moved to the city and started over from scratch. I got a job working at Jewel [Osco, a regional grocery chain] and then Boston Market, and I worked there for two years. One time I got to tour House of Blues. I started talking to the chef and I said, 'If you give me a job, I promise I'll be one of the best employees you have. I just want to learn.'" The chef was impressed with his initiative and offered him a job, and Julun rose through the ranks of the kitchen despite not having any previous kitchen experience. This in turn led to his current position as a chef at City Winery, a swanky Chicago restaurant and music venue.

One day a co-worker at the House of Blues came in with a pool bag slung over her shoulder and told Julun she played on a team in the APA. He was intrigued and agreed to go with her to one of the bars where she played with her traveling league. Although Julun's co-worker had to stick up for him

Reggie Julun took up playing pool relatively late in life but was quickly taken with the duties of a league organizer and tournament manager and has thrown himself into the bureaucratic aspects of the sport—all while playing on numerous teams in numerous halls. (Photo courtesy of the author.)

when the other players made fun of how badly he played, something about the game spoke to him. He wanted to continue playing, but if he did, he was determined not to be embarrassed like that again. He promptly joined a few APA teams and eventually started playing in tournaments. He would routinely get demolished, but this time the losses didn't sting because he knew this was part of the learning process and was more prepared to soak up the lessons learned.

As it turned out, I played Julun in my first-ever APA match in late 2019 when he was still going by "The Riddler," a nickname he bashfully admitted he gave himself because he's a fan of the character. He was just starting to feel the obsession really take root when COVID hit, forcing him to take a break but giving him time to realize his passion wasn't limited only to playing. More specifically, he wanted to get involved with the management side of the game, and once life got back to normal, Julun started helping Schaefer with his weekly duties in order to build up experience tabulating statistics, running tournaments, and managing the behind-the-scenes duties of league pool.

Julun had never done anything involving so much organization before, never thrown a big party or booked a concert, but he liked the hustle of making calls and setting schedules and working with bar managers and league players, and he realized he had the aptitude to keep details straight. This experience led him to try his hand at organizing, promoting, and running small tournaments, and one of the reasons he'd cut back the number of active teams he played for was so that he could run more tournaments, which he was then doing most weekends.

Julun gets his league fees covered and makes a little bit of spending money for his administrative duties in the APA, a bonus for doing something he says he would do for free for the sake of learning The experience has broadened his ambitions, or at least made him realize what's possible. He talked cautiously about eventually running a league of his own and expanding it to bars and schools. He also wants to do more events that bring in players from the Canadian and Japanese APA leagues and to create an app like Pokémon Go in which APA players could find nearby shooters for pickup games.

The interest in bringing pool to new audiences is in part related to how he grew up, though he didn't realize the connection at first. He just wanted to get better and liked learning the game, but he realized there weren't a lot of leagues in the area where he grew up, and most of the places with pool tables weren't particularly welcoming to unfamiliar faces. As he got older he began reading about Chicago's history and sociology and saw how the city's legacy of racial animus manifested itself in something as benign as pool.

Chicago has historically been a city of immigrants, and while the overlapping cultures and communities encouraged many positive cultural exchanges, humanity's unfortunate racial impulses mutated even further as the city grew increasingly crowded as more and more people arrived to take advantage of the city's rapid industrialization. Immigrants from Europe faced their share of discrimination and prejudice (the KKK, which was very active in Chicago, also targeted the Irish and Catholics), but they were also able to band together and be mutually racist against the city's Black, Latino, and Asian communities. As more than half a million Black southerners moved to Chicago between 1915 and 1940 to escape the dehumanizing Jim Crow laws of the South, these new residents were often met with appalling acts of violence (including beatings, race riots, and bombings) and rental and banking practices that segregated many Blacks in the city's South and West sides. Although these areas became hubs of Black culture and community, they also bore the brunt of the city's neglect, as they still do today.

Almost all aspects of sports and athletics in early Chicago were similarly infected by the racist ideology of the day. Sports, leagues, teams, venues, and athletes were strictly segregated, whether through de facto practices or out-right bans. Players from the old days recount that while White players could win in Black pool halls, a Black player who won in a White hall (assuming he was allowed to play in the first place) stood a good chance of not being able to leave with his winnings. Pool halls on the South and West Sides were often vital social hubs for their respective populations, places of camaraderie and mentorship. But there was also intense competition as players seized on their pool-playing abilities to boost self-worth and community esteem and perhaps earn a chance to pursue opportunities for financial and social advancement that might not otherwise be available to them. In addition, voter registration drives and grassroots organizing efforts often took place within the walls of the local pool hall, making them integral to the fabric of the civil rights movement. In fact, when Martin Luther King Jr. moved to the city in early 1966, visiting a pool hall was considered a great way to get to know his new community. King played against one of his colleagues, and reporters "went nuts, getting their own shots from every angle, making like they were filming *The Hustler*. . . . For days after, we heard nothing but reports of a new admiration of King."

I didn't have any firsthand experience with present-day pool playing on the South Side because my research for this book took place in central Chicago or the northwestern suburbs, but I did meet many players who grew up in or were presently living on the South Side (or various other historically ethnic enclaves). While acknowledging the many lingering consequences of the city's historical discrimination (such as insufficient employment opportunities, subpar schools, food deserts, and overzealous police), many players—Chinese, Salvadoran, Persian, Black—shrugged off questions about what their ethnicity meant to them as pool players, not particularly introspective about the topic or not feeling as if there was significant overlap between their background and the game.[1]

Julun agreed, as in most cases he thinks of himself as Reggie the Pool Player, a regular guy who just really likes to play pool. But having grown up in challenging circumstances, he could relate to other players with similar life experience, which is why playing in a league can inspire such deep feelings of place and connection. His interest in running a league was based mainly

---

1. Most people who played said they appreciate being able to rub shoulders and bond over the sport with so many different kinds of people; though not without its faults or the occasional race-based comment made under one's breath when someone loses, the accounts I heard were that the pool community has for the most part been quite welcoming.

on a desire to provide that same sense of community and on the ability of pool to create connections that transcend social divides.

Julun acknowledged he's had a few legal indiscretions, at one point spending a short time in jail, and a close relative of his is serving a lengthy sentence for a senseless murder he committed when he was young. Learning to cook and work in a kitchen revealed to Julun that he had the capacity to determine who he wanted to be, and pool became an even more powerful motivator to stay positive and productive. Holding community tournaments or introducing the game in schools or in after-school programs like the neighborhood leagues of yore could be ways to help people find direction through an engaging interest the way Julun did.

"You can change your whole life playing pool. I want to use the cards I've been dealt to make this a better place for the people who live here," he said. "I know I'm going to ask myself, 'What role did I play in this world to make it better for someone else?'"

Meanwhile, in the northwestern suburb of Arlington Heights, a man named Tom Van Eck had been asking himself a similar question. His basement man cave/pool den not only is home to his pool table and Superman memorabilia but also serves as the headquarters of the iCue, a teaching ball that Van Eck developed to help people learn different kinds of shots.

I suspected he must have his own laminator because tacked to his wall were laminated slips of paper with handwritten quotes from the online testimonials his iCue has received, and he had a thick stack of additional plastic-covered papers that hadn't been put up yet. He pointed to a paper on the top row. "'My game has improved so much. You have the best training ball on the market and the quality is just crazy,'" he read aloud with obvious pride.

The iCue is a standard white cue ball engraved with three concentric circles whose diameters measure 13, 20, and 27 millimeters, or the width of about two cue tips. Numbers run clockwise around the circles, with each number indicating where a player should hit to make the ball do specific things. Although there are plenty of other teaching balls out there, this system is purely of Van Eck's design. The iCue can be found in Chicago's pool halls and via online distributors accompanied by hand-written advertisements with his trademark rhymes, such as "Spin to Win" and "Improve your aim, improve your game."

Van Eck, a tall man with glasses in his late sixties, has been playing pool since he was ten and has been a fixture in the local scene for decades. It took little convincing for him to show me his invention in action. He moved a pile of posterboard and photos off the top of a 1905 Brunswick table whose felt was divided into three sections by bright masking tape. He pulled a small brace over his thumb and tightened it across his hand. He'd recently pulled a tendon, which made playing pool a bit painful, but he still played all the time, streaming his nightly practice-drill sessions on Facebook via a GoPro on a headband. Some of his videos are speed runs and others show his attempts to sink as many consecutive balls as possible, but in this case he wasn't filming and just wanted to demonstrate the practical application of his iCue system. "Ninety-five percent of tip contact is within the small circles on the iCue," he said. Balls spun away to the left and the right; some bounced off rails at unexpected angles, while others shot backwards upon contact with another ball.

The genesis for the iCue was Van Eck's work with area Boys and Girls Clubs. He saw that the clubs' pool equipment was in disrepair and felt that improving the equipment would help get some of the children out of their shells. "The kids are on the phones, playing video games," Van Eck told a reporter at the time. "Even 11-year-olds have smartphones. When they're hanging out, they're just sitting around a table looking down. They're not praying. They're playing with their phones."

He managed to obtain a top-of-the-line Brunswick Gold Crown table for one of the locations and began holding fundraisers that ultimately brought in about $26,000 to outfit a few of the clubhouses. He also provided free cues and table felt and began mentoring kids at the clubs. He drew some easy-to-use notations on a cue ball, and the children were blown away by what they could make the ball do with a few simple tricks. They begged him to show them more, and he earned himself the questionable nickname the "Pied Piper of Pool."

"[Pool] is a great way for kids to learn skills that extend beyond the table, such as physics, the law[s] of motion, patience, taking risks, about how to win and how to lose," said Cathy Malkani, CEO of the Elgin Boys and Girls Club, in an article about Van Eck's efforts. "Tom knows this, and he knows the importance of having such sports available for the kids. . . . People like Tom are making a difference in the world—one table and one child at a time."

Seeing how well this teaching technique worked, Van Eck got the idea to design and market a ball that would help players learn on their own. As it happened, he was finishing his career as a cola salesman and had hit all his sales targets during what happened to be one of the hottest summers ever recorded. He was given a hefty bonus check for his efforts and decided to retire early in order to give serious attention to his teaching ball, which he decided to call the iCue. The name is an obvious play on "IQ," he said, but he was also reading a biography of Steve Jobs at the time and liked the idea of a word with *i* in front of it.

His wife was amenable to his early retirement but said he could only use the money from his bonus check for work on his ball and couldn't touch any of the money they'd saved. He developed an iCue prototype but "wasted a whole year not showing it to anybody." He went to a pool tournament in 2015 and talked to Tom "Dr. Cue" Rossman, a pool professional and spokespersonality for the APA who hosts clinics and demos at APA events. Rossman was impressed with the iCue's design and encouraged Van Eck to show it off to the world. Van Eck bought a number of blank balls and got to work cranking out iCues.

The first balls had a complicated pattern with letters and numbers, and he had to deal with complaints that the ink came off when the ball was run through a ball wash. "Don't use my ball if you don't like touching your thumb to your mouth," he said, suggesting that players simply wipe the chalk off. But he simplified the design and switched to having his balls engraved by Jacoby Cues, a custom cue maker in Nekoosa, Wisconsin, known for its quality work.

Next, the gregarious Van Eck went out to sell the iCue. "It was like selling insurance—first you sell to all your family and friends," he said, and many of the pool rooms throughout Chicagoland have a small iCue section in their display cases. He sold his first ball outside Illinois in 2016, and the iCue is now available on Amazon and through distributors such as Pool Dawg. But he realized he needed a business partner if he wanted to expand his product further. "That's because," he said, looking around and dropping his voice to a whisper, "My wife doesn't give a crap about pool."

At that, Van Eck jumped up and went to a different part of the basement to retrieve a hand-penciled graph carefully charting the up-and-down sales of the iCue. The jagged but overall rising trajectory of the line was annotated with noteworthy sales such as the one-thousandth ball and a large run of balls sold to a distributor all at once. The trajectory rose significantly at one point in the middle of the chart, a change that Van Eck attributed to the "Jaden effect."

A few years earlier, Van Eck had come across the YouTube videos of a Baton Rouge eighth-grader named Jaden Dupree, who was going viral on YouTube mimicking the trick shots seen in *The Hustler*. He reached out to Dupree's management and arranged to have him feature an iCue in one of his videos and link to Van Eck's site in the video's description. Sales rose almost immediately, and Van Eck gave Jaden a dollar for every ball iCue sold regardless of whether they were purchased through a link from Dupree's videos. But at some point there was a dispute about how much Dupree was owed and the partnership dissolved. Van Eck's link was removed from Dupree's videos and, as the pencil lines on his graph indicated, his sales went down. A little while later Van Eck was at a convention and saw a vendor marketing a similar teaching cue ball. It turned out that Dupree had started hyping the rival ball, but Van Eck wasn't worried about it. Dupree had grown up by this point, he said—a thirteen-year-old pulling off wild trick shots is one thing, but watching an older teenager do it is not particularly special.

Van Eck continues to note memorable or important sales on Facebook and pursue new venues for the iCue, including vendors in the United Kingdom interested in the black ball and snooker versions of the ball. His wife maintains that he should pull back from the constant rhyming in his hand-drawn iCue advertisements, but he said he is drawing on his experience selling soft drink products and knows he needs a memorable edge if he is to stand out.

Van Eck works two days per week as a receptionist for a dentist that specializes in root canals but pool is his true calling, and no matter what else he'd been doing, he can't wait to get home and film some more basement speed runs and work on perfecting the iCue's marketing campaign. He recently sold his 5,107th ball, a hustle he's glad to still be making, and he continues to work with local organizations to inspire a dedicated and wholesome interest in pool.

"I'm not very religious, but so many times the guy upstairs said 'Go there, go here' with pool," Van Eck told me. "It's all come full circle. It *is* a circle!"

A little while after meeting with Van Eck, I caught up with Reggie Julun back at City Pool Hall as he was shooting with one of his teams and holding court with players who'd come up to say hello. One of those players was Mauricio, the captain of a 9-Ball team and a wiry, energetic guy who was one of the fastest pool players I'd ever seen, unafraid to hop up and stretch across the table for a shot.[2] Julun and Mauricio worked together at City Winery, and Mauricio said he was soon going to be a father for the first time. He was tremendously excited for the birth but was also planning to keep playing pool as close to the due date as he could. A tournament was coming up, and he would be very disappointed if he missed it. But, he added, the mother of his child would understand: she was one of his teammates.

"Good luck in the next couple of weeks!" I said as we parted.

"I got mad skills, my boy!" he yelled back. "Mad skills!"

---

2. Players can lean all over the table if they want, provided they keep one foot on the ground.

I was referring to his impending fatherhood, but I think he thought I meant playing pool.

Julun explained that he was in a transitional phase again. He'd left City Winery after being told by management that there was essentially nowhere else for him to go at the restaurant. There was no point in staying if he wouldn't be challenged, and since then he'd challenged himself to try to make pool a more viable money maker. He had increased the number of tournaments he was hosting, but earnings depended on how many people signed up to compete. Sometimes he'd make $50 for six hours of work and sometimes he'd spend more money running the tournament (including transportation, food, and a drink or two) than he made from it. A few times he was forced to cancel a tournament when not enough people signed up.

He did have a line on what amounted to a dream job: a management position at Nick's Billiard Academy, one of the spots where Julun spent a lot of time learning to play and regularly hosted tournaments. The position at Nick's would draw on his managerial experience in the kitchen and seemed to entail what he was doing now with tournaments but included a real salary. He talked about the possibility in such a way that he almost avoided talking about it directly, as if to not jinx his chances.

A few weeks later, however, Julun told me that the position at Nick's hadn't been in the cards, for, as much experience as he had running tournaments and working in kitchens, the people in charge didn't feel Julun was quite ready to helm the whole operation. According to Julun, they'd wanted to start him at a position lower than he felt he warranted, and the possibility fell apart from there. There were no hard feelings; he went back to City Winery and kept up his tournament schedule, team commitments, and league obligations as steadily as ever.

When asked if he ever got sick of pool, the customary question I ask of people who spend an inordinate amount of time on the sport, he replied, "No, I really don't. We all need something to care about or there's no meaning to life."

Julun, like Tom Van Eck, was a workaholic, and each was even more energized when it came to working on something as personal as pool. Julun did a quick calculation of how much time he devoted to the sport.

"I put in at least forty hours per week on pool," he said. "I'm a part-time worker and full-time pool player!"

CHAPTER 12

The Last Hurdle to Vegas

The Arlington Lanes Citywides

Jackson May, a bartender at Surge Billiards in Logan Square and a member of numerous Chicago APA teams, was positively distraught.

It was July 25, 2021, and the tall, bearded, broad-shouldered twenty-eight-year-old former kickboxer was pacing around the edges of the pool room at Arlington Lanes, a classic midwestern bowling alley in a shopping plaza with two estheticians, a computer repair shop, and a pancake restaurant, and incidentally not far from Tom "Mr. iCue" Van Eck's basement workshop. His dangling earring bounced as he walked.

May, a 3 handicap who plays for the Billiard Men, was playing in the Arlington Lanes Citywide, the culmination of the Chicago APA's spring 2021 session and the final Chicagoland tournament that would send players to the 2020–2021 World Pool Championships. Though the Billiard Men played at Surge Billiards in Chicago, Chicago APA league operator Brad Hall had been hosting his tournaments in the suburbs for years for reasons of logistics: There is food, there is parking, and there are abundant tables, eight in the main room and five more in a bright but weirdly lit side room.

The Arlington Lanes edition combined the winners from the 2019–2020 APA seasons and the 2021 sessions that had been played so far. The Billiard Men were off to a great start ("Ryan [Morse] did some work out there—he slayed some 7s," said teammate Ricardo Cagnetta) and the team had been playing well enough against current opponents the Black Pearls that May didn't have to win all the games of his match to earn enough points to secure the team's victory; he only had to get on the hill. May has a quiet confidence that underscores his obvious strength, but that aura faded fast when he fell into a slump he couldn't seem to get out of.

Especially painful was the easy 8 ball he missed at the end of the third game, which cost him the match and meant that team captain Eli Mancha would now have to play the next match. Even if Mancha lost his match and ended the team's chances, May would blame himself for the snafu.

"I've been trying to say nothing but affirmations to myself," he said, as he continued to pace. "'*You're a good player. You're a good player.*'"

The atmosphere at citywides is markedly different from the one at weekly league play. Shots are more deliberate and players more subdued; observers stand quietly at respectful distances from the table, rubbing their chins or quietly sipping drinks. The tension was indeed palpable at Arlington Lanes, and the air resounded with increasingly intense exhortations as the evening wore on. Genuine tears were shed when a year of hard work just couldn't get a team past the final hurdles.

"Gah!" one guy said as he watched his teammate get squashed. "This makes my dick itch!"

The 2021 Arlington Lanes Citywide began on Saturday, July 24, and the final matches were under way by 3:30 p.m. on Sunday. Hall said he never got burned out even after being an operator for decades. He walked through the crowds with a low-key air of avuncular joviality, chatting with patrons, some of whom he'd known for about as long as he'd been running his leagues, and many of whom he'd played on teams with many years earlier. Hall's league had 260 teams before COVID but now stood at around 240.

Former APA league owner and current assistant Gregg Taylor was likewise in his element at Arlington Lanes, a bit more effusive than Hall and delivering nonstop wisecracks and old pool stories in his gravely smoker's voice, the same as he did when he'd help Ross Schaefer in a similar capacity.

"I've seen people get served with divorce papers in the middle of matches," he said, before talking about how he once saw a table collapse mid-game because one of the legs wasn't set properly. (The shooter was given a foul and the game continued.) He laughed at the memory before pausing to peel the lettuce and tomato off a chicken sandwich. He asked a passing server to bring him mayonnaise specifically from a jar. The sandwich had come with mayonnaise packets, but he didn't trust them for some reason and insisted on getting the condiment straight from the source. "I'm probably the leading cause of death of chicken," he noted, before taking an un-mayonnaised bite.

Taylor, who is from Chicago, has been playing pool seriously since he was nineteen, with gambling a big part of his initial interest in the sport. He previously worked as a repo man and was somewhat used to people giving him trouble and threatening him, but still, getting stabbed twice because of pool was not pleasant. "The first time was for $563," he said, pointing to scars on his head and arm. "This is from pool, too," he continued, pointing to a gnarled pinky. He still got some shit from time to time as a tournament operator, and someone was once so mad at his ruling that he told him he'd piss on his grave. "I told him, 'Son, you lack the intestinal fortitude to wait in line that long to piss on my grave,'" he said. "But there will be port-o-potties at my funeral!"

Nearby, Jackson May had stopped pacing and was watching with rapt attention the game Eli Mancha unexpectedly found himself playing.

"Oohhh, that was all nerves," Taylor said when Mancha failed to make a shot.

Mancha tried to stay calm as he switched to a more defensive style of play, but his opponent was able to get out of the traps he set and make some impressively complicated maneuvers. "How did I escape? With difficulty. How did I plan this moment? With pleasure," as Edmond Dantès said in *The Count of Monte Cristo*.

Mancha has a large red 3 ball tattooed on the top of his left hand, a number and color that have always been lucky for him. Another talisman, a piece of tiger's eye stone, is in his pocket when he plays. "I try not to wish harm on people, but sometimes I think, 'miss that shot!' And they will." Mancha evidently channeled the right amount of superstition, and the match began to turn around. The table steadily emptied, and his last shot would be diagonally across the table, about as long a shot as possible. Mancha pushed down any doubts he might have secretly had and took what appeared to be an effortless tap at the 8 ball.

The ball sailed down the table straight and true and sank what was intended, and his teammates all jumped out of their chairs with an explosive cheer. The Billiard Men had taken out the Black Pearls to become the top performers in their league and the winners of a trip to compete in the World Pool Championships in Las Vegas.

"I was making 'em sweat. All the way down to the last game," Mancha said. "It was a do or die situation. Ask me to do that again and I probably couldn't."

May beamed with relief that his loss didn't have any lasting consequences as Eddie May and Adina Fried clapped him on the back. At that moment, Eddie looked happy but slightly strained. He was psyched to see his brother win but was only semi-joking about being a bit jealous of the victory—he still had never personally won a trip to Vegas. His brother, on the other hand, had been playing for less than three years, was a few handicaps below him, and had already won a trip, as had Fried, more than once. Still, Eddie would be going to Vegas anyway, and he knew there were plenty of places to get his hustle on beyond the walls of the Westgate Casino.

A round of shots for the Billiard Men, whose victory at the Arlington Lanes citywides secured their trip to the 2020–2021 World Pool Championships. (Photo courtesy of the author.)

After posing as a team for a photo for APA social media, the Billiard Men threw back some shots and went over the highlights of the match they'd just played. The Black Pearls were packing up their gear, and one member said he wasn't interested in a post-game interview.

"Now is not a good time. I'm way too upset right now and I know I would say something bad if I talked to you," he said, his lip trembling as he headed out the door.

I walked back over to the victors.

"The worst part about being a league operator is saying 'I'm sorry' to the guys who got second place," Taylor said.

Fortunately, this wasn't a message the Billiard Men were going to hear. They were bound for Vegas, and they'd certainly earned the trip.

"This team's amazing!" Mancha said. "We got a *squad*, man!"

CHAPTER 13

Excited and Terrified

Preparing to Play in the
World Pool Championships

A man named Cesar Morales has been called the "best pool player that never was." In 1985, at Reds in Houston, Texas, hundreds of players congregated for a tournament. The young and unknown Morales seemed to come out of nowhere to work his way up the ranks and take the $10,000 top prize. But when some fans asked for his autograph, Morales's signature gave him away—it turned out he was Efren Reyes, a god among pool players. Although his name was known, his appearance was still a mystery in the pre-internet days, allowing him to compete under the radar without anyone being the wiser.

In today's carefully regimented world of the APA, however, score sheets, photo IDs, algorithmic modeling, and a large digital presence in the form of photos and social media mean there was little doubt about the identities of those who would be playing in the relaunched, delayed-session-resolving, extra-large 2020–2021 APA World Pool Championships. Just as other winning teams were doing across the United States, the shooters with the BB Cues, the Billiard Men, Kickin' Like Bruce, and Wake and Break began coordinating time off work, time away from kids, rides to the airport, and the logistics of reuniting as a team in Las Vegas. The teams also kept up their regular schedule of APA league play since the championship typically is held in the middle of the regular fall session, which pauses only briefly to accommodate Vegas-bound teams.

Like many players, Brian Hale of Kickin' Like Bruce wanted to get some practice in before heading out to Vegas. Though he grew up playing pool, Hale's first love was basketball, and he played in a local league for more than twenty years, eventually taking on mentorship and coaching roles. But his playing days came to an end when he annihilated his ankle in the middle of a game. The injury was hard to deal with because it was a reminder that we all, unfortunately, have to age, but pool helped fill the basketball-shaped void as he drew on the same mindset and discipline that helped him excel in basketball to deliver on his team's expectations. The competition in Las Vegas would be on "3½′ × 7′ Valley Panther ZD-11 or Cougar 93 tables with Mercury Ultra cloth, standard size pockets, and either Valley Supreme or Ridgeback rails" and would use Aramith Premier 2¼″ balls and a Valley Cougar cue ball." Although no hall in Chicago had this exact setup to practice on, the seven-foot tables at City Pool Hall would do the trick, Hale said. "If you make it to citywides, you've gotta put in some time."

Captain Adina Fried of the BB Cues was likewise trying to hit the tables every day in the week or so leading up to the tournament. "As captain, I feel like I really have to perform," she said, noting that she'd recently been quite hard on herself. "Alison [Lewis] is better than me, but when she beat me the other day, I got really pissed off. But then I realized that's a good thing. I need to push myself." Vivian Ramos said she wished she had practiced more, but work left her no time to do so. "I haven't even packed yet," she said, in part because she was "excited and terrified" of what lay ahead.

The Billiard Men's Eli Mancha had been watching old World Pool Championship matches on YouTube to get in the right headspace. He found himself wondering what the announcers might say about him if he made it that far and had to put the videos on mute so he didn't further stress himself out, since he was also impatiently waiting for the team's shirts to be finished. Team shirts are crucial for team cohesion, identity, and pride, and the team could hardly go to the tournament without them. The Billiard Men's 2021 design would feature an image of Billiard Man, a Gundam-like cartoon whose pieces of armor were all pool balls. They were slated to be finished in the next day or two.

Mancha also knew that a few players were going to have their handicaps bumped up, which would change the balance of the team's cumulative handicap and the strategies they'd employ in Las Vegas. The games they played at the World Championships would no doubt affect handicaps further. "It's going to be hard to have that conversation," Mancha said, as he knew a lineup change was coming and he'd likely have to ask a teammate or two to step back from the team in favor of a lower-ranked player. Going to Vegas would only solidify their bond as a team, meaning that it would be even tougher to have this conversation when the time came. "The highest[-level] players have been friends the longest," he said. "And two of them are dating."

It's nominally an all-expenses-paid trip, but this doesn't mean that players don't have to fund part of the journey. The shooters on Wake and Break, for example, were given $600 each, and Sonia Aujla was able to secure a sponsorship for the remainder of their expenses through a friend who worked for a Bitcoin ATM network. The company gave them some money to put their logo on the team's shirt and make a single social media post hyping the company. Duly outfitted, their cue sticks were polished, their bags packed, and they were on their way.

League operators around the United States were likewise getting ready to go to the World Championships, often to serve as floor referees or provide administrative help. Ross Schaefer and Gregg Taylor sometimes do this, but neither made the trip in 2021. Instead, they fielded calls and helped arrange flights and lodging from back in Chicago. Taylor said he's gone to Vegas so many times he's practically a resident there, though he doesn't go as often anymore because he doesn't like to board his cat. Las Vegas is trying to be too family-friendly these days anyway, he remarked—you can't even smoke in the hallways anymore, just the casinos. But whether they're physically at the championships or not, Taylor and Schaefer make sure they are reachable at any time to help players with rules and logistics. "The Peppercorn," Taylor said. "That's where you've gotta eat."

To be sure, league operators are in for a stressful week. Most teams arrange to stay for the duration of their respective tournaments in the event that they make it to the finals. But that also means the majority of players must make arrangements to come home early when they get disqualified sooner than they were hoping to. That's where the league operators really get to work, arranging and rearranging travel plans for dozens if not hundreds of individual players. In order to do this, the APA works with airlines to reserve a certain number of seats with no names attached to them. Players are assigned one of these seats when it's time for them to go home. "Southwest hates us because we've got eighty people on the plane and change arrangements all the time. They probably add a $20 surcharge when they hear it's the APA," Taylor told me.

Going to and from the tournament can be one of the most frenzied parts of the experience. Taylor has regularly dealt with people missing flights or going to the wrong airport, and he once saw an APA player get hit by a car. "From that point on, I arranged for buses to pick people up at the airport," he said with a grimace. Very occasionally he must mediate issues that arise between players and hotels. Once, some players were kicked out of their hotel for continuously smoking weed and blowing smoke into the air vent that poured directly into the room of the elderly couple next door.

"If you get in trouble, they'll embarrass you on purpose. They'll perp-walk you through the whole hotel," Taylor said.

Approximately sixteen hundred miles away from the APA headquarters in St. Louis, a phalanx of box trucks and semis packed the loading areas of the Westgate Casino starting about a week before the World Pool Championships. The trucks carried the hundreds of pool tables, displays, set pieces, officials' tables and scaffolding that enable and adorn the APA's main event.

Lighting is the first thing to be set up, with the hundreds of trapezoidal overhead pool lights hung from specially installed scaffolding hanging from the ceiling. Then, the hundreds of pool tables that take up the unbroken acres of ballroom space are all brought in individually by handcart. As a former mover, I can tell you that moving pool tables is no joke. Handcarts certainly make it easier, but there's still the matter of picking the tables up and putting them on the carts, pulling them a great distance, and navigating them in and out of the truck and through the twists and turns of the convention center.

Once the tables are set, "pipe and drape" fixings (curtains hanging from waist-high, museum-style rope partitions) make each table into its own squared-off zone of competition with its own enclosed seating area. Dozens of vendors set up their booths and displays, many of which have large-scale sets and decorations and pool tables and whose walls are made of fencing in order to more easily hang goods. Additional box trucks and semis deliver hundreds of boxes of pool merchandise and the food, drinks, and toiletries necessary for thousands of people converging on one spot. Countless banners, posters, and other APA decorations throughout the convention center thoroughly brand the event.

The 2020–2021 edition would be the seventh time the World Championships were held at the Westgate Resort and Casino. They were previously held just down the street in the Riviera Hotel, as they were in 2010 when the *Guinness Book of World Records* declared it to be the world's largest pool tournament, but the Riviera closed in 2015 and has since been demolished. The Westgate began hosting the tournament in 2016, when the event was rebranded from the APA National Team Championships to the World Pool Championships in order to include the teams from Canada and Japan.

The resumption of a regular schedule of preparation and competition in the months following the COVID-era lockdowns made for a sense of giddiness and excitement around the APA offices. The pandemic had made a significant dent in the APA's membership, said marketing director Jason Bowman, reducing it from 250,000 to 220,000 members, and players felt as if they'd lost access to their entire community. The APA helped league operators and bar owners navigate the process of obtaining government grants to keep their businesses afloat, and the league pulled through relatively unscathed. "We were fortunate we were able to hold it together and have enough leagues come back quickly and avoid any layoffs, which was really important to the company," he said.

Still, being at the World Pool Championships in an official capacity for the entire duration of the tournament can be an endurance challenge. For Bowman, it's at least two straight weeks of announcing games, putting out fires, arbitrating disputes, attending to company duties, and then going back to a lonely hotel room and talking to his family on the phone when he has a few spare minutes. But when Bowman lands in Las Vegas and looks around the familiar halls of the Westgate, he's always proud to return to his other home and carry out the unique duties of a pool organizer and emcee.

"It's actually kind of sad when it all gets torn down at the end, almost like we were never here," he remarked, noting it only takes thirty-six to forty-eight hours to pack the whole thing up. "But it's a good thing the first APA tournament didn't have 300 tables—that would be an overwhelming event to coordinate with no experience."

Airports around the country soon began seeing an increase in passengers with long, thin bags slung over their shoulders. Thousands of pool players descended upon Las Vegas from all corners of the United States, eager to engage in billiardian combat. They were far from their friends and families and regular concerns and were going there to finish what they started. They were among their peers and their people but also among their foes, and a distinct, sphere-shaped fire could be seen burning brilliantly in their eyes.

PART III

Viva Las Vegas

CHAPTER 14

Entering the Anthill

The 2020–2021 APA World Pool Championships, Part 1

A man from Headland, Alabama, named Jace Grant strolled down Elvis Presley Boulevard with his teammates and friends to make the half-mile walk from hotel-casino Circus Circus to the Westgate Resort and Convention Center in Las Vegas. They appeared tiny against the gaping expanse of a parking garage under construction, the pieces of a new edifice taking shape where the Riviera, the previous home to the World Pool Championships, once stood. Grant was wearing the characteristic quiver-like pool bag and was striding purposefully but also leisurely, excited to hit the tables but enjoying the process of getting there. Grant was in Las Vegas, of course, for the 2020–2021 championships, and he and his team The Pocket Pirates were some of the 14,000 players from around the country converging on Las Vegas from October 21 to October 30, 2021.

"My therapist knew I played pool and said playing would be good for me," Grant said, thrusting out his right pointer finger, which he'd lost in an accident six months earlier. "I'm still getting used to it but playing pool does help." His first exposure to pool in Vegas was when a friend invited him to tag along on a trip he'd won to play in a tournament. "He told me he wanted to give me the Las Vegas pool experience in case I made it here someday and had to shoot. And here I am."

We'd struck up a conversation while waiting at a crosswalk, and that immediate conviviality was the way it went all over the northern end of the Las Vegas Strip. Any ride in an elevator, stroll through a casino, or trip to the bathroom was instantly enlivened by a conversation with a fellow pool player, a bond that opened the door to a lengthier conversation about strategy, equipment, or a terrible call the referee had made. My conversation with Grant

The Westgate Resort and Convention Center. The World Pool Championships are held in the ground-level convention center, which extends beyond the bottom right of the picture. (Photo courtesy of the author.)

followed a similar trajectory as we approached the intersection where Elvis Presley Boulevard meets Paradise Road. Across the street, the vantage point obscured in part by palm trees and an unusually large 1960s-style marquee, was the Westgate Casino and Convention Center, the place the players had been dreaming about and the place where their dreams would live for the next eleven days.

The Westgate is somewhat far from the glitz of the Strip proper and is relatively unadorned compared to well-known establishments such as the Luxor or the Bellagio; it's much more like an airport convention center than an opulent resort. The compound's hotel is a humongous white Y-shaped building, and the convention center extends like a massive industrial complex off to the right.

Hordes of pool players disembarked from the tram that runs up and down the Strip and made a stop at the Westgate's Jetsons-like platform while an unending parade of cars, vans, and taxis disgorged players into the crowd milling about outside. The movement was constant, the people like ants outside an anthill with massive glass doors. The crowd extended down the side of the building and into various patios and shaded areas along the exterior of the convention center. There wasn't a moment during the entire tournament when these areas weren't filled with smokers; "the Surgeon General is nowhere to be found in that gangway," as one writer put it.

Teams from all forty-eight contiguous states and a few Canadian provinces made the trip. (The usual Japanese contingent couldn't make it because of ongoing COVID-19 concerns.) Teams represented major metropolises such as Los Angeles, Boston, and Chicago, but most teams came from places such as Leland, Florida, Oswatomie, Kansas, and Eureka, Missouri.

The World Pool Championships were happening at the same time as the Indian National Finals Rodeo and Electric Daisy Carnival, a rescheduled rave that would bring three hundred thousand additional people to the city that weekend. The confluence of events necessitated some rerouting of airport shuttles and made for a dearth of taxis and Ubers, leading some players to arrive directly at the tournament instead of first checking into their rooms at a different hotel. That's what happened to Adina Fried and Eddie May, who had just arrived at the Westgate, luggage in tow, to head straight to watch May's brother Jackson play with the Billiard Men.

The energy was even more frenetic inside the Westgate's main entrance, with countless inhabitants rushing every which way to different parts of the complex; anywhere you wanted to go required dodging waitresses, tourists, and fellow players and navigating around clanging machines and gambling tables. A hallway off to the left of the main room led to the tattoo parlor and wedding chapel standard to any Vegas hotel, and this came just before the gift shop of Barry Manilow, who was the Westgate's artist-in-residence at the time. But the vast majority of people headed down the gilded and tiled hallway to the right, past an Asian fusion restaurant and into the convention center proper.

Fried and May plunged into the scrum of players, officials, and fans, subsumed into the crowd that surged through a succession of rooms lined with tables and tents and awnings and displays and then onto the cavernous ballroom floor, where almost all of the tournament games would be taking place. "I need some table therapy!" one t-shirt put it, a sentiment everyone clearly shared.

The number of pool players increased the deeper we got into the convention center, with many browsing the booths of vendors, distributors, and cue manufacturers who brought tools and equipment to do onsite repair, their spinning machinery filling the air with fine dust. MiniMania, the unending series of small-scale tournaments that players could sign up for, occupied its own room and had a line of participants winding around dozens of tables and flanked by large display screens with the results of the numerous overlapping

Each room of the Westgate Convention Center is packed with tables, booths, and players, who use computer terminals to follow brackets and get table assignments. (Photo courtesy of the author.)

mini-brackets. In the hallway between rooms was a frog-themed massage booth that offered the "Rubbit Rubbit" technique to alleviate pool player stress, while all the vertical display surfaces of the table next to it were completely covered in layers of pool gloves in every possible color, sports team, and style. The woman behind the table, who made the gloves herself, would be huddled over her sewing machine for the duration of the tournament. When she wasn't making new gloves, she was repairing those that were worn through. "Sorry, I'm really busy right now," she said. "Maybe we can talk later."

Eddie May and Adina Fried passed all of this without much comment and arrived at the grand foyer to the main tournament room. There was a burst of natural light from the floor-to-ceiling windows that looked out onto the smoking section on one side of the building and, on the other side, onto a patio where overpriced Sysco Systems food was being sold from grill stations under fancy awnings—$13 for a burger, $8 for a hotdog, $4 for a bag of chips, and $3 for a single banana. In the foyer was a pool table with a small set of bleachers surrounding it that held numerous exhibitions by trick shot artists Florian "Venom" Kohler and Tom "Dr. Cue" Rossman, who provided technical insight via shot clinics but also life advice via spiral-bound booklets intended to help players become "Student[s] of the Game . . . and *Life*!" May pointed out with some admiration that although Dr. Cue was never one of the all-time great players, he has been able to make a living for decades as a pool personality, an influencer long before the internet age.

The crowd's shoulder-to-shoulder sojourn finally ended at the main ballroom, at the furthest end of the convention center. This was the giant central chamber and primary playing field of the World Pool Championships. It was almost time for the opening ceremonies that would kick off the 8-Ball tournament, and Kohler briefly stopped his demo as the crowd filed by. It was easy to pick out people who were new to the event by the way their stride would abruptly slow when confronted with what lay beyond the ballroom's doors.

They couldn't help it—it was truly glorious.

Inside was a pool city, a pool landscape, a surreal pool fantasy. It was like City Pool Hall multiplied by a hundred, a dive bar by a million. The room was hundreds of feet deep and even longer wide and entirely open, uninterrupted by pillars or dividing walls. Scores and scores of pool tables stretched to the horizon, each illuminated by its own light. The tables were so numerous and so expertly aligned that the rows looked like something in a funhouse mirror. "Somebody plumbed that shit *straight*," one player said.

Wide avenues divided the room into manageable neighborhoods of pool tables with hanging banners indicating the table numbers below like addresses so that competitors could find their game. Each table had its own seating area for players and fans, and most were already occupied by teams from all over the country assembling gear and shooting around and settling in for a long day. It was a massive, collective game that, as Scottie Smalls says in *The Sandlot*, didn't have a beginning or end; it just seemed to go on forever.

"This is where we play, baby!" said one APA player loudly to nobody in particular.

Mobile bars staffed by affable bartenders were set up at the intersections of the avenues that spanned the halls.

"What do I owe ya?" one player asked the bartender, two drinks in small plastic cups sitting on the counter between them.

"Owe me? Well, you don't owe me nothin'—but you owe the hotel eight dollars!"

They both laughed.

Fried and May swerved around the crowds of players and people carrying drinks and broke off to the right and down one of the avenues, suitcases still in tow. The Billiard Men's Christina Arce walked down the path toward

The main ballroom of the Westgate Convention Center has hundreds of tables stretching from one end of the room to the other for the championships. "Somebody plumbed that shit straight," one player observed. (Photo courtesy of the author.)

them with two plastic bags filled with drinks and snacks. She met up with Fried and May and showed them to the table where the Billiard Men would be playing their first game.

Fortunately, the team's shirts had been finished in time, and everyone was wearing a t-shirt or sweatshirt with the image of Billiard Man, the only exception being Ricardo Cagnetta, who was neatly dressed in his customary polo shirt tucked into khakis. Spirits were high. It felt like a vacation with purpose, an adventure with a sense of possibility in the air. Captain Eli Mancha handed out temporary tattoos with the Billiard Men's name as peppy songs played over the loudspeakers, an inoffensive mix of music™ that included everything from NSYNC to 3 Doors Down to the Bee Gees. "The music calms me; it helps a beat keep going in my head," Arce revealed. "It helps me not see my opponents. I don't focus on them at all."

Along the back wall of the ballroom was the oddly high podium from which judges and officials observed the proceedings. Giant flat-screen monitors placed throughout the ballroom informed players of the tournament's rules and etiquette. Because this was still the recovery phase of the pandemic, one sign advised that "Masks must be worn except if actively shooting," a phrase that could've been worded a little better given our present reality. Players wore masks only because they weren't allowed to play if they didn't (with no shortage of feelings expressed about this requirement), but for some teams, masks were another way to fly their colors: Eli Mancha's mask bore an image of the valiant Billiard Man.

The music from the loudspeakers came to a halt and a hush descended over the room. Hats were removed as the U.S. and Canadian national anthems were played and then a series of APA officials came to the podium to say encouraging words about why we were all there, how hard the teams had fought all year, and how great it was seeing so many players doing the thing we all love after such a weird and difficult year. "Good luck and good shooting!" an official said a few minutes later, and with that, the opening ceremony drew to a close, the music began playing again, and it was time for the first games of the 8-Ball tournament at the 2020–2021 APA World Pool Championships.

"It's not fun to be bad at this," Fried said as the Billiard Men got ready to play. "Nobody enters a tournament to get kicked out right away."

CHAPTER 15

Pool Dreams and Pool Nightmares

The 2020–2021 APA World Pool Championships, Part 2

Following the cracks of the opening breaks, the Westgate's giant hall echoed from morning until late at night with the sound of pool and the cries of competition, sometimes even between teammates.

"This is bullshit!" yelled one player whose captain had just made the decision to play a more reliable shooter.

"Listen," the captain said. "Ritchie's been on a roll all week. The last thing he needs right now is his own team second-guessing him."

The woman and a friend who'd been standing next to her in solidarity crossed their arms and stomped off together in protest. The captain rolled his eyes and turned back to his team. Only a few games in, and already tempers were flaring. Ironically, the team's name was Luck Runs Out.

Nearby, another player watched his teammate get trounced by a 7.

"He didn't even get a chance to shoot!"

"Yeah, he did. He broke!"

The BB Cues got together for a pep talk once they'd assembled as a full team in Vegas. They'd all arrived separately and weren't all staying in the same location, with only Christine Degrange staying at the Westgate because she was competing on numerous teams that week and it was much easier to take an elevator downstairs than to walk or take a cab to a different hotel. Alison Lewis said she would not be staying in the Westgate in order to avoid one of the more unpleasant aspects of the tournament: cigarette smoke. "I promised myself I would never be one of those ex-smokers that talks shit on smokers," she said. "But think about it—there are hundreds of teams with eight people on a team and 70 percent of those people smoke."

Smokiness of the venue aside (Lewis's estimate was low; it was more like 90 percent of players smoked) the BB Cues handily won their first two matches, dispatching the Queens of 8's and then the Ladies straight to pool player hell, including an impressive set of games by Vivian Ramos, who'd finally been able to visit Las Vegas because she'd made it there by playing pool. It turned out that "Ladies" was not the opposing team's real name but a stand-in to replace "LFG," the name they'd given when entering the tournament. The APA doesn't allow acronyms such as LFG because the letters could stand for something rude, which, in this case, they did—"Let's Fucking Go"—which is why they had to be replaced with something generic.[1]

The BB Cues' games were scheduled such that they had twenty-four hours off following their second win. Part of that time was spent hanging out as a team at a poolside cabana until their match against JR's Queen Bees the following evening. The BB Cues were energized by their time off and left the Queen Bees fatally encased in their own propolis, but from that point on the women barely had a non-pool-playing moment to themselves. Their next day would see them playing at 9 a.m., 1 p.m., and 5 p.m., a schedule that could result in twelve straight hours of pool.

It would be an exhausting schedule for sure, but it was a successful, encouraging start.

"We might actually win," Fried allowed herself to think. "We have a good fucking lineup."

Wake and Break—the team from Chicago, not the Wake and Break from Florida, as there were two teams with that name—lost their first match against Alcohol and Bad Decisions but stayed alive in the loser's bracket against the Magic City Shooters from Hueytown, Alabama. Jay Vatanagul put himself up to play their opponent's best player, and although he lost, he did get on the hill and earned a point, a sacrifice that freed up teammates to play people who were better matches for them. The Chicagoans ultimately were able to put a hex of their own on the team from Magic City and resurrect Wake and Break from the loser's bracket and back into the main tournament for a second chance at glory.

It was a lucky save after a disappointing start, and I mentioned to Sonia Aujla that she'd once said she has "pool dreams and pool nightmares," a phrase that had stuck with me. She laughed and said that was definitely still true; simply being at the tournament made it difficult to sleep. "I keep having dreams that I oversleep. I wake up every hour and want to run for the door," she said. But so far she'd managed to make it to all their games on time and

---

1. The APA website has a list of hundreds of previously banned team names to help teams avoid this sort of problem (or just because it's hilarious). Personal favorites include The Jo Blobs, Mount-N-Dew Me, and Hairy Helmet and the Cooters.

was determined to prove that a rocky start wouldn't define their 2020–2021 performance.

Captain Eli Mancha of the Billiard Men made sure he brought a few extra pairs of contact lenses with him to Las Vegas. He'd never switched over to glasses because he didn't want to have to adjust his pool game, one of many captainly stratagems he'd exhibited so far at the tournament.

"I had a talk with the team about taking it seriously," he told me. "It's always the strong players who take their skills for granted. 'I can play hungover,' they think, but not really."

"No mercy for people who get too drunk or miss their flights!" chimed in Jackson May from off to the side.

The Billiard Men's first match against Just Make It (the match Eddie May and Adina Fried dragged their suitcases to immediately after they landed in Vegas) ended up being a bye, and the team handily won their second match, against Eight's Enuf. The third match pitted them against the Shot Takers, a team from Arlington, Texas, that had one of the better team shirt designs: a skeleton gripping an 8 ball, which gave off old-school POG vibes.

Unfortunately, Jackson May accidentally sank two of his own balls a few games in, tying the pair at 2–2. Mancha tapped his foot nervously, but Cagnetta blew May a kiss from the sidelines as Joe Cocker's version of "With a Little Help from My Friends" played overhead. The combination seemed to work, and May easily swept the rest of the match.

Ricky Torres was up next, noticeably tense but trying to stay in the zone and able to seize on the chance to take his opponent down when he missed a crucial shot. "Tonight's gonna be a good night! / Tonight's gonna be a good, good night!" pulsed from the loudspeaker, and the dulcet tones of the Black-Eyed Peas instilled the confidence Torres needed to hand the team the third victory in a row. Although a celebratory drink was certainly in order, most of the teammates opted to call it a night and went back to their rooms to maintain their disciplined mindset.

Table assignments often weren't given out until the match was about to begin, frequently leading to a mad dash of players across the Westgate to their tables. Teams learned of their table assignments via computer terminals set up throughout the convention center, which provided access to a database of all competing teams and a full set of tournament brackets. The program interface took some getting used to, and I was happy to help some older players find their bearings and navigate the system once I figured it out myself. (A phone app version was also available but was even more confusing and had most information locked behind a paywall.) The terminals were crucial for helping me stay up to date on the Chicago teams' locations and progress, but when I wasn't watching one of their games (or whatever interesting match I happened to come across), I wandered the convention center and took in the sights and sounds of the tournament and perused the latest wares on the pool scene.

The many stalls set up around the perimeter of the rooms of the convention center were filled with thousands of pool tools and accessories ranging from elegant pool bags to chalk cubes in vibrant colors, high-quality ferrules and innovative tip tools, and teaching balls à la Tom Van Eck's iCue. Pieces and parts, including the many different kinds of couplings used to join the two halves of sticks together, were displayed in boxes and baskets and piles like spices in a bazaar. Surprisingly, while there are a few recurring designs, manufacturers like to use proprietary couplings in the interest of branding and exclusivity. Vendors thus sold coupling adapters used to make a shaft fit with an unrelated butt, though this does add a bit of noticeable weight to the cue that might throw off a player's technique.

A contingent of raffle ticket vendors walked endless loops around the convention center with signs advertising prizes taped to the ends of the cue sticks they held aloft. The most common item to be raffled off was a pool cue, and each raffler adopted a personality to sell tickets, from hard-partying stoner chick to down-home grandfatherly type to a woman wearing a taco hat and a cow costume and carrying a sign that said "If you buy a ticket, you can milk the cow and take a picture if you want." King of them all was perhaps the only person in the world whose persona is based on selling raffle tickets: His pitch included striking a pose with both arms crossed in front of him to reveal the message "Rise or shine / it's raffle time" tattooed on his forearms.

Such high-level salesmanship impressed an attendee named Charlie, who'd come from Missouri to support his wife's team. He stood along a wall of the convention center and in one hand held a melting iced coffee and in the other, a bulging plastic bag. He'd promised himself he wasn't going to pick up any supplies or merchandise during the trip, and the bag he had with him contained all free swag. But, he said, he was definitely going to buy a Whyte Carbon shaft when his wife's student loan check came through. Whyte Carbon was a new manufacturer of futuristic-looking cues, and Charlie was already wearing the shirt he'd been given for buying raffle tickets at the firm's booth.

Anyone who wasn't wearing a Whyte Carbon or other pool-equipment-related shirt was wearing his or her team's shirt. Almost every pool shirt had

Many vendors bring their tools to the tournament to repair competitors' pool equipment and accessories onsite, including cues, tips, bags, and gloves. (Photo courtesy of the author.)

Players also have an endless selection of pool-themed clothing to choose from, including the countless designs and styles offered by Hustlin USA. (Photo courtesy of the author.)

No pool room is complete without a wall full of pool-themed art, from artistic shots of balls across a table to more light-hearted fare such as portraits of famous personalities ready to play the game. (Photo courtesy of the author.)

the same aesthetic, which is to say completely (and endearingly) devoid of any graphic design sensibility whatsoever. Most appeared to be designed with clip art and featured dad-joke pool puns or phrases about how much pool has taken over the wearer's life. Some, like "MARA: Make Amateurs Rack Again" or a design with both Blue Lives Matter and Christian iconography, suggested a team's cultural perspective, while other shirts simply displayed the sponsoring bar's logo under the team's name. There was also an abundance of pro–Second Amendment and "American Guardian" apparel on display, which many tournament players had just picked up from a far-right Christian conference they'd just come from in Tennessee. "Sometimes you don't appreciate how much you're representing Chicago until you leave the city limits," Reggie Julun said when he went to the World Pool Championships for the first time the following year. (In my opinion, the best shirt design at the 2020–2021 championships could be found at the official APA merch stand, which is in a small, enclosed cinderblock room like a snack bar under a high school football stadium. The APA shirt had a "man evolving from monkeys" graphic that ended with the man crouching to shoot pool.)

Almost all non-team merchandise was similarly devoid of a designer's touch and lacked any inter-brand cohesion whatsoever. California-based Hustlin USA was one of the larger and more popular vendors, with the bulk of the company's merchandise having the word *Hustlin* embroidered onto miscellaneous polyester items in the plainest of serif fonts. The booth seemed to have far too many items—there were easily seventy-five designs on dozens of kinds of apparel, from polo shirts to jackets to items made of strange athleisure fabrics to skimpy ladies' wear—and I felt bad that the company had spent so much money getting things made that nobody would buy. But what did I know? Everywhere you looked, and increasingly throughout the week, countless players had the Hustlin USA logo visible on one or more pieces of clothing, and I would notice a ton of the company's gear back in Chicago once I knew to look for it.

Rubbernecking at one of the booths, I barely avoided colliding with a pool player in a motorized scooter who then almost hit the guy behind me as he swerved to miss me. A bag filled with merchandise listed precariously to one side behind his seat.

"Don't worry—I won't hit ya!" the driver said.

"Don't worry—you'd win!" the other guy said.

We all laughed and went our separate ways.

Soon enough, it was time for some players to start heading home.

The first from Chicago to fall was Wake and Break, whose journey to the World Pool Championships had begun almost two years earlier in the pre-COVID fall session of 2019. Wake and Break had already experienced some serious emotional ups and downs having going into and out of the loser's bracket, and their run was brought to a close by Who's Next, a squad from San Antonio, Texas, who would themselves get knocked out not long after. The members were not happy about the loss but recognized that there was no single culprit for their less-than-stellar performance. Losing their first match hadn't helped their psyche, and they just couldn't seem to let it go.

"I've seen people rip into teammates when they lose, but I don't want that kind of atmosphere," Vatanagul said.

Sonia Aujla had optimistically budgeted for up to five days in Sin City, but the team had played only three matches across two days. On one hand, she was already there in Vegas and might as well enjoy it, but on the other, there was no need to incur additional expenses if she didn't even feel like hanging out. Besides, regular league play was still going on, and Aujla had her non-Vegas teams to attend to back home. Soon enough, the members of Wake and Break began working with their league operators to arrange flights back to Chicago.

The BB Cues were still doing great, and the Billiard Men looked spry and refreshed as they marched over to table 319 for their match against the Bounty Hunters, a team from Jackson, Michigan, that was composed almost entirely of current and former prison guards. As it stood, the Billiard Men were in 128th place.

"We're a better team," Eli Mancha said. "That's what I'm banking on—pun intended. I was here six years ago and got to this point. My immediate goal is to make it past this point."

Eric Case, who was with the Bounty Hunters, said the team was down 5–0 their first night, "but we like to come back. We tightened the pockets of our tables at home to make sure our shooting was more precise." This was Case's fourth year with the team, which was coached by his father-in-law Richard Jenkins Jr., who had made it to Las Vegas for the first time in his more than thirty years of playing in the APA. Case disputed something I'd often heard in Chicago: that Chicago teams in particular are known for their pool talent. He told me he'd never heard that Chicago teams were any better or worse than anyone else, but he did concede that the Billiard Men were playing well.

A few people from the Shot Takers, the team the Billiard Men had beaten the day before, were on hand to watch the match.

"They were hungry. They wanted it more," one said. "They knocked us out of the competition; we might as well cheer for them."

"As long as they shot like they did yesterday, they should be fine," added another.

A few hours later, the match had gone on so long that Sudden Death was declared. Ricky Torres had one chance—one game—to win or lose the match. His palms were sweaty and he was no doubt ready to throw up his mom's spaghetti, and a few of the Billiard Men made "calm down" gestures as Torres took a deep breath. A few great shots later, he'd opened up a clear path to victory.

One final ball.

Pling.

"Fuck yeah! That's what I'm talking about! Fuck yeah!"

It was unclear who yelled it, but everyone on the team felt the same excitement anyway. Though the team had called it an early night the night before, making it this far was too exciting not to stay up a bit later to celebrate.

Later that night, once most people were free of their tabletop obligations, a crowd of APA folks gathered to watch a country singer named Sam Riddle and his band play from a small stage near the Westgate's casino floor. Riddle was wearing a big cowboy hat and an oversized sterling silver necklace and looked like a high school quarterback posing for the cover of a romance novel. He was backed up by a solid set of musicians, including a pleasantly weathered guy who looked like he'd been reincarnated as a chain-smoking guitar player following a previous life as a chain-smoking guitar player.

A group of women pool players stood at the front of the stage and swooned as they held their drinks aloft.

"This pool crew is a lot of fun," Riddle said, his voice twangy and melodious. "My backing band is called . . . 'Eight Ball Corner Pocket.'"

The women laughed.

Riddle then started to make a comment about Joe Biden, but a serious-looking man in the crowd—presumably his manager—made a hand-across-the-throat gesture and shook his head. Riddle laughed, the attempted comment passing without notice (though it almost certainly wouldn't have offended anyone in attendance). He thanked the crowd for their time and the band geared up for their next number, playing on amidst the eternal din of slot machines and swaying of pool players eager to get some respite from the rigors of the past few days of competition.

CHAPTER 16

The Toll of Too Much Pool

The 2020–2021 APA World Pool Championships, Part 3

Prompted in equal measure by excitement and stress, the already elevated levels of smoking and drinking became even more intense as the tournament progressed. People got sweatier, stinkier, and more disheveled as time went on, wandering around and staring into the middle distance, fueled primarily by fried food and snacks. "People only leave to eat, sleep, and shower—some more than others," as Gregg Taylor once put it.

One woman with bags under her eyes was sitting outside the Westgate smoking a cigarette and drinking a beer. She was telling her friend that her husband, who was on her team, pushed her down in their hotel room and ran off with the $1,500 they had brought to sustain them for the week. She locked him out of the room but was awoken in the middle of the night by intense pounding on the door. He had almost immediately gambled all the money away, just as she expected. "I told him, 'Go fuck yourself!'" she said. He ended up passing out in the hallway, but the pounding resumed at 8 a.m. "Go *FUCK* yourself!" she screamed again, but this time it was four security guards. Someone had called her team's captain and reported her husband for acting like a jackass at a nearby bar, and security was there to check on things. The husband came back in the middle of this visit and put up a drunken struggle that required six additional security guards. Eventually, she agreed to let him back in the room to pass out, where he presumably still was when she was relating these events. "I haven't eaten in three days," she said, her arm shaking as she took a drag on her cigarette.

One pool player reported winning and losing more than $21,000 gambling in a single night, while another found himself surrounded by security guards in the Westgate casino in the middle of the afternoon. "I swear to God I'm not a thief!" he screamed, suggesting that the security guards speak with APA officials to verify his good standing as a human being and someone who, in twenty years of playing, had never missed paying his dues or green fees. But the security detachment remained unmoved, and the man was marched away. It was unclear what prompted the confrontation, and his fate remains unknown.

I dabbled a bit in gambling in Vegas myself, though I know nothing about the pursuit and was too intimidated to sidle up to a live table. I instead opted to play a few hands of blackjack on an electronic machine in the dingy sub-casino next to the equally dingy Circus Circus, where I was staying. Whereas some parts of Vegas are the equivalent of an expensive shopping mall expanded to Disneyland proportions, some parts, such as Circus Circus's satellite casino, are sparsely populated betting parlors inhabited by people lurking around in the middle of the night (myself included). Given that ATMs in Las Vegas casinos dispense $100 bills and gambling tables accept these bills (and credit cards), the $150 I budgeted to mess around with disappeared into the table and was lost forever within fifteen minutes, a pricey lesson quickly learned.[1]

There were noticeably fewer people inside the Westgate convention center by this point, with the majority of teams disqualified and either already returning home or wandering around elsewhere in Sin City. Some players, worn out but staying out of trouble, sat in the bleachers and looked up listlessly as Dr. Cue did trick shots and the teams that were still in the tournament marched to the main ballroom, legitimately solemn, their matching shirts and

---

1. It's interesting that, despite the massive sports betting complexes in every Vegas casino/resort, with IMAX-sized screens showing footage and statistics of practically every sporting event going on at the time, pool for a long time has been conspicuously absent. Many say that's because Las Vegas bookies swore off pool following the events at the 1991 International Challenge of Champions.

The Challenge of Champions was an eight-person mini-tournament played at the Mirage in Las Vegas that was to be broadcast on ESPN. Bookies picked favorites and started taking bets, with Hall and another player being favored 3:1 to win the whole tournament. Competitor Mike Lebron was given 20:1 odds, and suddenly there was a flood of bets on him to win. According to a significant amount of analysis since then, it appeared that Hall purposefully missed the two final shots of his championship match with Lebron, shots that shouldn't have been missed by a pro. The implication was that Hall and many of the other competitors in the tournament conspired to let Lebron win and then collect their earnings from the underdog bet. It is unclear whether the 1991 Challenge of Champions payout was ever made in full, and in subsequent tournaments, participants had to sign a form essentially affirming that they would play the game honestly. The Challenge was hosted in Las Vegas until 2016 and was occasionally featured on ESPN, though Las Vegas bookies have refused to take any lines on the event since the first edition.

Players need a rest—any way they can take it—after days and days of playing pool. (Photo courtesy of the author.)

pool bags making them look like some kind of regiment.[2] Nine-Ball players trickled in as the beginning of their tournament drew closer; you could tell who they were by their color scheme: black, white, and yellow, the colors of the 9 ball. The various members of Kickin' Like Bruce who'd already arrived were in the main hall shooting around on open tables.

The Billiard Men were up against The Stumble Inn 8 from Godley, Illinois, in a battle for 65th place. The team was huddled in one corner of the observation area next to their table. A few of Mancha's players had had their handicaps raised by a point because of how well they'd been playing in the tournament, and this had the much-dreaded effect of throwing off his rotation. "My 6 and 7 are now out, so I have to field my 5s against 2s *and* 6s," he sighed.

Ricardo Cagnetta was first up, and it didn't go well. The piles of plastic cups, ice buckets, coffee cups, bags, and cans on the team's table grew larger still as the Stumble Inn 8 began to pull ahead.

---

2. Teams could perhaps lean on Rossman for celestial favor. In 1987 Rossman had a vision telling him to bring the Gospel to these players. He is the author of "Rack Up a Victory: A 'Special' Manual for Your Billiard Journey," a free, faith-driven manual that is part pool instruction and part spiritual guidance. As the founder of RACK Vision Outreach, Rossman uses pool to connect players with God. The ministry's motto is: "To win is great. To play is greater. To love is the greatest." Rossman and his wife Marty ("Ms. Cue") also offer morning Bible studies at various pool events.

"I wish I could just jump into someone's body and shoot for them," Ricky Torres said.

"I hate this game, I really do," said someone playing for Stumble Inn 8.

Mancha went back to the hotel to freshen up, and when he got back, he was let in on some strange news. Rumor had it that the person he was scheduled to go up against had recently been raised from a 5 to a 7. Mancha's eyebrows shot up. A bump that significant was likely an indication of sandbagging and should've triggered some alert in the APA's system. But the game was apparently going to continue as scheduled, and Mancha went on with the match, figuring it was only a matter of time before the matter would be looked into and the match stopped. He and his opponent took turns shooting and returning to their corners like recovering boxers.

"I can't watch this shit anymore," the Billiard Men's Pierre Kasiansky said, stroking his beard.

Before long, however, the Stumble Inn 8 had the full advantage, and the match came down to its final shot. There was a sense of the inevitable in the air and sure enough, the player for the Stumble Inn 8 sank the 8 ball, defeating the Billiard Men for good. Mancha sighed, his visage melancholy, "made so perhaps by the world as his mind would have it in comparison with the world as he sees it," as John McPhee wrote.

Once the pique of the loss was absorbed, Mancha fixated on the particulars of how it happened. Given the handicap raise, the match simply shouldn't have moved forward, he decided, and he tracked down some floor reps to plead his case. Unsatisfied with the outcome, the team went higher up the food chain and sought a floor manager at the officials' tables along the back wall of the ballroom. The tables were draped with black cloth and were so high up that players had to crane their necks to talk to the officials, like something out of Kafka's *Trial*. Their ruling was just as unfavorable as the one cast down on Josef K: the Billiard Men had already signed the forms conceding that they'd lost, and there was nothing they could do to reverse it.

"I signed it with a pencil—give it back to me and I'll erase it!" Mancha said.

It only got worse. Not only had Mancha's opponent been raised two points, but so had someone else on the team, an occurrence that Mancha felt absolutely should've induced a pause in the proceedings. But the Stumble Inn 8 were already playing their next round against Brandon 2. Brandon 2 ended up beating Stumble Inn 8 and went on to play Here We Go Again, but higher-ups in the APA evidently got wind of what was going on and finally stopped the proceedings to look more closely at the teams' statistics. The results of the review were shocking: The APA didn't find anything problematic with Stumble Inn 8's tournament journey, but it did find that Brandon 2 had its own set of questionable handicap raises that led to allegations of possible sandbagging. Closer investigation led to Brandon 2 being disqualified for cheating and being asked to leave the tournament grounds. A huge DISQUALIFIED appeared in the computerized brackets next to their name, the only team that year to earn this dubious distinction, and the team would have to meet with an APA tribunal later on for further castigation. But because the shenanigans seemed to have ramped up during Stumble Inn 8's match against a verifiably sketchy team that was disqualified, the APA invited Stumble Inn 8 to the 2022 World Pool Championships to make up for the confusion.

Though the APA determined that the team that beat the Billiard Men didn't appear to have been sandbagging, Mancha still felt that the investigation was lacking and was let down by the way it all played out. In fact, he said he was told surveillance footage confirmed that one of the ostensibly low-ranked players on the Stumble Inn 8 was leveling 6s and 7s in the MiniMania tournaments—proof positive from his perspective they were sandbagging, but he had only heard of this alleged footage through the grapevine and couldn't confirm it for himself. Either way, he couldn't enjoy himself when the team went to dinner later that evening. "Everyone was having a good time and getting shitfaced," he said, but he was constantly on the phone texting Chicago APA league operator Brad Hall to see if he had any influence in getting the team reinstated. Hall did what he could, to no avail, and most of the Billiard Men collected their things to head back east, though Jackson May was determined to stay in Vegas and make the most of the trip.

At least six friends vacationing in Las Vegas came to see Kickin' Like Bruce, meaning the team had a noticeable entourage for its first match against Rhode Island's Team Badrinath. Wayne Wong tried to get in some last-minute practice before he left Chicago but said he felt like he'd peaked in skill level 5 since most of his practice was on his regular league days. But he wasn't fazed by the bustle of the approximately 150 games going on around him in Vegas, and he exuded confidence on the tournament floor. He walked away victorious not long after.

"Wayne talks shit but he shows out," Bo Lee said.

Kickin' Like Bruce displaced I Don't Care later that evening and won the only match it played the following day, against The Yellow 9-Ball. This success raised co-captain Wong to a 7, adding the expected handicap complications and possibly keeping him out of competition for good. The team started fresh the next morning at nine with a victory against Get Over It! (who no doubt had to follow this advice) and then won again against Wait for It.

Kickin' Like Bruce's final match of the day was against Scratchers, and with a 7 p.m. start time, it meant Kickin' Like Bruce had been playing pool for

Players, some excited to learn and others taking a break from competition, watch as Tom "Dr. Cue" Rossman gives one of his many scheduled demonstrations in the lobby in front of the main competition hall. (Photo courtesy of the author.)

the past ten hours. The match dragged on until Sudden Death was invoked, doubling the value of each ball and lowering the overall score needed to win.

"I'm terrible at defense," said teammate Cynthia Tang. "It always looks better in my mind."

Despite the handful of memorable shots and the resolute trouncing they had delivered in earlier matches, this wasn't going to be their year. Like Wake and Break, everyone played decently, nobody dropped the ball, but then again nobody really did anything heroic, either, and by this point they were far enough along in the tournament that there would be no second chances if they lost. Indeed, it was right in the middle of their tournament run that Kickin' Like Bruce's luck finally ran out and the Scratchers sent them back to Chicago.

"I would've liked at least to make it one more round," said Jennifer Mui. "But I think we did pretty good for it being most of our first times."

Though Kickin' Like Bruce had been disqualified about halfway through the time they were scheduled to be there, nobody opted to go home early. The novelty of being able to bring along some of their longtime friends (and wives) for the first time was a fun new dynamic to share for a team that had grown up together. In an earlier era, as they all could remember quite well, they might have let themselves go a bit wilder than they were willing to in the present. But they traded shenanigans for eating—"lots of eating"—and a sense of appreciation for being there that counterbalanced a trip cut short.

"We don't get mad at each other—we just get drunk!" Hale said.

Whereas some pool players were partied out and others were bummed out, fans of Chicagoland pool still had a few teams to root for and would in fact have to pick sides. Both the BB Cues and defending national women's champs the Apocalypsticks had worked their way through the tournament brackets until they were scheduled to play each other in the semi-finals. Adina Fried couldn't believe they were actually at that point—the winner would go on to the women's finals and the loser would take third place. Everyone on the BB Cues knew someone on the Apocalypsticks, and the team held a meeting about how best to get in their opponents' heads. There were subtle tricks that could be employed, but the best bet was simply to go out and play as seriously and calmly as they could.

As could be seen at many matches at the World Championships, phones were set up on tripods to livestream the action to players back home. These cameras captured Fried playing first against Darlene Dantes—and taking a loss.

"This is it, it's all over," Fried thought.

Alison Lewis was up next and was clearly a bit nervous, losing some games but regaining her composure to come back and take the match. The team was fully in sync at this point, and the conclusion came hurtling toward them sooner than they'd expected when Christine Degrange took down her opponent with ease.

"There's no crying in pool," one Apocalypstick said, and the team hugged the BB Cues on their way to collect their $2,000 third-place check.

Fried couldn't believe it, but then she corrected herself—of course she could: They'd worked their asses off for this, taken their losses like champs, and kept playing together like a team. The next match was, incredibly, the 2020–2021 Women's League APA finals, and Fried vowed not to let any sort of doubt creep into her mind. They'd be up against We're Feelin' Lucky, a team representing the mean streets of Huntsville, Alabama.

Some people from the audience stumbled by as the BB Cues were packing up.

"I thought I was supposed to be the drunk one!" one friend said to another.

Fried smiled in their direction. After a long day of shooting, she too could use a drink.

CHAPTER 17

Live from Pool Dawg Arena

The 2020–2021 APA World Pool Championships Finals

Adina Fried had played nine matches in the championships so far, more than anyone else on the BB Cues. The finals would consist of up to three matches, and as captain, she decided she would be playing in the finals as well. The decision also hadn't been an easy or popular one to make.

Alison Lewis, for her part, knew she wouldn't be tapped to play and was okay with it because it was a bit too much stress and attention for her liking anyway. Christine Degrange and Teresa Jimmerson were both reliable, solid players, earning them both a spot on the finals team. By process of elimination this meant that Vivian Ramos would also be sitting out the final match. Though Ramos had played well throughout the championships and won a number of her matches, Fried felt that she tended to retreat into herself when she lost, which in turn affected both the way she played and the mood of the team.

Fried hid out in a bathroom to psych herself up to break the news, expecting the decision to have consequences beyond the present disappointment. A few minutes later she walked up to Ramos and got right to the point. Ramos made a cogent case for why she should be one of the players in the championship match, but the team had come too far to defer to politeness; Fried told her sympathetically but firmly that she wouldn't be playing. Ramos nodded. The team walked into the finals arena a bit more quietly than might have otherwise been the case.

Whereas almost all matches at the 2020–2021 World Pool Championships were played in the Westgate's main hall, teams were plucked from obscurity for the finals and placed under the glowing lights of the Pool Dawg Arena, a room renamed for the occasion after one of the event's main sponsors.

The hallowed ground of Pool Dawg Arena awaiting the next pulse-pounding finals match. (Photo courtesy of the author.)

Instead of hundreds of simultaneous matches watched by a few people each, hundreds of people would be watching a single match from the bleachers surrounding the table, not to mention the viewers tuning in to watch the livestreamed match on the APA's YouTube channel. Fried's parents would be watching on their phones while on vacation, and pool halls back in Chicago would stream it on their TVs.

A small army of people moved around the playing floor getting the match ready to go: a referee, suited APA officials, camera operators, hotel staff, and somewhere off to the side, a strong, mysterious, intelligent, and truly handsome writer taking notes in a small, weathered notebook. Overlooking it all were two well-dressed announcers in an enclosed booth who had been providing commentary on every finals match so far and would be narrating the Women's Championship as well.

"It's ladies night here in Pool Dawg Championship Arena—it's all about the ladies," intoned Jason Bowman, sitting beside his co-host, pool personality and APA league operator Ewa "The Striking Viking" Laurance.

"I'm a little partial to the ladies' division," Laurance said. "I love it, I love the ladies, their excitement."

Fried was used to the bustle of the average league night and had long since stopped being self-conscious about playing in front of people. But here, she felt herself going back and forth between being hyper-aware of the situation and adrift in a more Zen-like sense of just being. "I wasn't any more calm than the other rounds, but I kept telling myself I have nowhere else to go," she said.

The teams gathered around an APA official to get a rundown of how the event would proceed.

The match would be played to five points, and scoring would be according to the APA standard: two points for a victory, one for getting on the hill, and three for a shutout. The teams nodded in agreement behind their required facemasks, which gave the proceedings an even more solemn air. Two players went to shake hands, and one accidentally grabbed the other's wrist.

Fried lost the lag, which meant that Katie Ottaway of We're Feelin' Lucky, a 4 handicap like herself, would break the first rack. Shockingly, Ottaway's first attempt was a miscue, which was harmless, penalty-wise, but not great for her psyche. Nothing was sunk on the next break, and Fried quickly hopped up to shoot. But both players appeared to be plagued by nerves; there were a few missed shots before Ottaway was able to sink three in a row.

Fried and Ottaway each took a game, with the third a test of patience owing to a cluster of balls that required a "smart little cat-and-mouse game" of trading safeties. Fried, however, steadily gained the upper hand.

"She hit that as well as you can hit it, ladies and gentleman," Laurance said when Fried's grind paid off. "Well done."

The score was now two games to one in the BB Cues' favor.

As the match went on, Fried couldn't help but peer over at herself on the giant monitors showing the livestream, watching herself watch herself and wondering what the commentators were saying about her. At one point she was worried that they were saying she was playing too slowly, but they in fact noted that Fried was shooting too quickly.

Bowman briefly cut the tension by announcing that the BB Cues would like to give a shout out to Alison Lewis's kids and husband, City Pool Hall, and Fried's dogs Bruce and Willis.

"If the pups are watching, I'm impressed," he laughed. "If we can entertain the domesticated animals of the world, we're doing something right."

Bowman and Laurence kept the narration going as the fourth game began, offering analysis, personal anecdotes, and bits of trivia about each team, who before the match had filled out a questionnaire with interesting information about themselves. The commentators' buoyancy and creativity were particularly impressive because they'd been at it for more than a week straight, narrating the finals along with attending to PR obligations and other APA business, not to mention that they would continue commentating right up until the very end of the tournament, even as other APA staff began breaking off and heading home. Laurance, a league operator in North Carolina, also had to manage the affairs of the teams in her league that were playing in Vegas.

Back on the table, Fried was having a rougher go of it, and the score was even at 2–2 when Ottaway barely avoided scratching on the 8. In the future, Laurence said, the APA needs to install a mic above the crowd to better capture all the oohs and aahs.

Ottaway "kissed ice water" as she walked up to the table for the fifth game, but the break didn't pocket any balls. Fried sank a ball and opted for a safety. "You have to play within your skill level," Laurance noted—the final is not the time to be a hero.

Ottaway sank two in a row, but the third shot dogged around the rim of the pocket and jumped back out onto the table. A quick timeout consultation with Alison Lewis helped Fried plot out the best course. She knocked the 9 ball into a far corner and then pocketed the 14, bringing all the action down to one end of the table. The final 8 ball, that gleaming black sphere of destiny, was tantalizingly close to the corner pocket, and the 3 ball Ottaway left on the table posed no encumbrance.

"It looks like she's going to walk away with this one as long as she keeps hold of the cue ball," Laurence said.

Fried looked down the length of her cue, an extension of her being. The match was over seemingly before she shot, or at least before she realized it. The crowd cheered, cluing her in to the fact that the BB Cues had decisively won the first match of the women's national championship, netting two of the required five points.

Fried stepped toward her team to celebrate but remembered to turn around and first shake Ottaway's hand. She then took a quick jog around the playing floor and high-fived anyone within reach. The announcers took a break as the BB Cues' Christine Degrange got ready to face Barbara Teal (both 5s) in a race to four games.

In the interim, livestream viewers were treated to an absolutely bonkers run of commercials.

First was a wordless Pool Dawg spot that consisted of alternately sloweddown and sped-up shots of gleaming, rotating, and somehow erotic pool equipment against a clinical white background. One shot lingered over an embroidered pink leather pool case in such a cinematic way that it looked like a country-western version of *The Matrix*, and another shot showed pool gloves going onto hands as if the wearers were preparing for a brutal fight.

Next was an epic commercial that hyped APA membership with the most triumphant music possible, a strings-heavy orchestral bombast of the kind that plays as someone is fighting to save a city. "Las Vegas: for most, the ultimate party destination," the narrator intoned. "A place to run wild and leave the routine behind. But for a pool player, it's so much more. Take your Vegas fate into your own hands today; realize your Vegas *destiny* tomorrow."

Next was another ad for the APA, this time with the quality of a local commercial, a group of friends at a bar taking turns saying why the game is better when they play together. The commercial break then concluded with a lengthy slideshow with jubilant electronic music of pictures from APA leagues around the country.

"All right, and we're back here, folks," Bowman said. "Christine Degrange with the break for the BB Cues. She won the lag and is a skill level five."

Judging by the walloping Degrange was delivering right out of the gate, the women's finals wouldn't go on very long. The BB Cue simply would not let Teal make a shot and quickly won the first three games.

"Sometimes the pool gods are against you," Laurence said. "There's not much you can do about it. You just got to try to hope that they change their mind and give you some opportunities as well."

As many players noted, being ranked a 4 or a 5 in Chicago was like being ranked a 6 or a 7 in other cities—the level of competition was just that much more intense in such a densely populated locale. The gulf between their respective abilities was very apparent, and the fourth game just as easily turned to Degrange's favor. Soon enough the final ball was on the table, a ball that if sunk would give the BB Cues enough points to effectuate a shutout. That meant three whole points added to the two they already had for a grand total of five points, the number they needed to win it all.

"This is for all the marbles—and to forever be labeled a champion," Bowman said.

Degrange knew the pocket she wanted to go for and put a marker down next to a corner pocket.

The ball zig-zagged down the table off a couple of rails toward its destination.

The audience gasped.

But the ball stopped short; Degrange didn't hit it hard enough. The match continued.

A few more gasp-inducing tradeoffs later—Teal missed a sure shot as well—things were back on track for Degrange. The 8 ball was inches from the pocket and the cue ball a few inches from that.

"I don't want to say I'm a gambling woman these days . . . well, I kind of am a gambling woman, but I would bet this is it," Laurence said.

Degrange marked her pocket.

It was so quiet you could hear a beer open.

A beer did in fact open.

Someone coughed.

Degrange took a deep breath.

She took her shot.

The room erupted in cheers as the ball dropped in. The rest of the BB Cues rushed from behind the barrier and onto the playing floor to hug Degrange, who'd just gone 4–0 against a seasoned 5.

"BB Cues, folks, Chicago, Illinois. They are your ladies champions," Bowman said.

As the team was hugging, a masked table assistant came to the table and pushed the cue ball into a pocket, closing the match for good.[1]

Back in Chicago, there was a collective cheer as friends, family, and league colleagues watched the BB Cues pull off a national victory.

Fried herself couldn't believe it and felt as though she couldn't move. The BB Cues had fought their way to the absolute apex of APA play and could now verifiably say they were the best ladies' team in the league. They would soon have an $11,000 take-home prize and a hilariously heavy and oversized trophy to prove it. (Fortunately, the APA graciously offered to mail the cumbersome trophies home.)

A hand yanked Fried cartoon-style across the room to do a quick post-game interview.

"It's a beautiful freakin' day, dude, and I can't believe it. It's very surreal and I'm very, very excited," she said.

After giving a shout out to her dogs, Fried gave heartfelt cheers to the women in her league.

"I'm so proud and thankful and honored that you guys choose to spend your weeks with me," she said. "You're in this space with us, all of you are here with us now, I love you all and love my whole team. Thank you all!"

Fried was thrilled by the team's accomplishment, but she also knew the standards of everyone on the team had changed. Going to—and winning

---

1. The video may be viewed at https://www.youtube.com/live/sohDL3dnsRI?si=DQ ZQ0-gtuoM9q-CV.

The BB Cues, 2020–2021 Women's League national champions, moments after their victory, with the giant check to prove it. (Photo courtesy of the author.)

in—Las Vegas was clearly within their reach, and there would be a new level of seriousness as they attempted to maintain that momentum in the upcoming season. She knew that her choice to sit some players out of the finals match had created a new dynamic she'd have to navigate, but she shrugged it off and let herself get caught up in the well-deserved excitement. Her only regret, she would later say, was not taking the pile of cash and making it rain. After all, how often do you get a chance to stand under a shower of money you just won, and won by dominating the APA World Pool Championships?

PART IV

Hopes Re-Racked

CHAPTER 18

An Expression of Barbarian Temperament

Getting Back to the Tables

> Cultural theorists, anthropologists, and psychologists all note leisure's central place in any society or culture. The time has come to recognize leisure's full historical potential to test existing theories and pose new arguments about society and culture at-large. I use billiards as a vehicle to propose ideas about American society and culture as well as to examine the sport's reflection of American society and culture.
>
> —Kenneth Cohen, "Billiards and American Culture"

In February 2022, a few months after the close of the 2020–2021 World Pool Championships, Russia invaded Ukraine in an old-school show of imperial ambition, shocking the world with its cruelty and brutality. One night around that time I was on a bus to Surge Billiards and imagined the streets of Chicago turned into a war zone, the storefronts and cars reduced to burned-out shells, people forced from their homes, and unimaginable danger and discomfort around every corner. The violence in Ukraine was going on amid a war between Ethiopia and Eritrea, anarchy in Haiti, growing right-wing fascism around the world, and various other horrific conflicts, and when I got to the pool hall, my cynical frame of mind caused me to fixate on the sense of competition that was the main point of almost every game and sport we play for fun.

Sporting has been called an "expression of barbarian temperament" and the "social safety valve that replaced the frontier" because it gives us a chance to harness the primal truculence at the center of our being. The ancestor of a pool cue is a spear, and the precision required to sink balls is no doubt a reference to the survival techniques we honed in order to defend our tribe. While pool is not deliberately violent like football or hockey, it does play on the same impulses, and I had to wonder if something as seemingly innocuous as athletic competition helps stoke a mindset that in turn reinforces the primeval feelings of territoriality that can mutate into something much more threatening.

But when I walked into Surge, nobody seemed to be consumed with thoughts of impending doom or was driven to a competitive frenzy against people from another neighborhood. Instead, everyone happily went about their normal routines, shooting pool, eating, drinking, hanging out, and entertaining another bid to make it to Vegas.

Indeed, as any athlete will tell you, far from stoking arbitrary divisions, games and sports foster connections by providing a way to bond over our shared impulse to compete and enabling us to do so in a controlled, rule-based environment whose outcomes we understand and accept. A game like pool allows practically anyone with an interest to excel regardless of age or traditional athletic talent, the acts of learning and teaching deepening a sense of camaraderie and belonging.[1] Whether people were in retreat from fears of society's imminent collapse or simply enjoying each others' company, the pool world was a comforting place to be, a reminder that the whole point of life is doing what you love with the people you love as often as you can.[2]

While some players were perhaps still a bit disappointed about not making it as far as they'd liked in Las Vegas, it was difficult *not* to get hopes up again, buoyed as they were by having earned passage there in the first place. The Billiard Men, Kickin' Like Bruce, Wake and Break, and the BB Cues thus had one of league pool's elite challenges before them: Could they make it to Vegas for the second year in a row, or, in the case of the BB Cues, hold onto their national title?

---

1. Games such as pool and ping-pong are great because incredible agility and strength aren't prerequisites, but depending on how they're played, they can also create some hilarious frustration in competition. I saw a ping-pong tournament once that didn't have any age divisions, and a player in his forties was trying hard not to lose his cool against his ten-year-old opponent, who was kicking his ass despite barely being able to see over the table.

2. That spring in Chicago also saw the Austin McGreal Memorial Tournament, an event held at City Pool Hall and organized by McGreal's family as a way to say goodbye to a husband, father, and friend. As McGreal's stepson Tom explained, McGreal started playing pool relatively late in life, and when he found City Pool Hall, he realized he'd found another part of himself. The hall was decorated for the tournament with large printouts of photos and mementos from different eras of his life, from his love of photography and jazz to becoming an attorney at age fifty-eight. His stepfather was typically a stoic, private man, Tom said, but when he was playing pool he was social, familiar, and unburdened, happy to spend hours playing and mentoring new players. The best way to commemorate his life was to throw a big pool tournament in his name, and that's what they did.

CHAPTER 19

A Toehold out of the Funk

Catching up with Wake and Break and Kickin' Like Bruce

There were approximately forty teams playing in the 2022 Chicago Central APA citywides, which took place in June 2022 at City Pool Hall. This year, the event combined the winners of the Surge, City Pool Hall, and traveling leagues in order to promote cross-league competition. This combination offered a new challenge, as part of the strategy comes from knowing your opponents and how they play; here players would go up against people they'd never seen before.

A bell from the kitchen dinged constantly to indicate food orders were ready, and servers walked by with trays full of steaming cups of coffee to keep people alert. For similar reasons a player openly sniffed a white substance off a Metra card in the bathroom before heading back out to shoot. "Why you high-fiving? It ain't over yet!" another person yelled to his teammate across the room.

Reggie Julun was playing on a team in the tournament while also helping people find table assignments and updating the day's bracket in a notebook that was curling up at the edges with hand sweat and extensive pen marks. He'd recently moved on again from City Winery and had gotten a new job working in an upscale liquor store. As with the curiosity that drew him to pool, he found himself increasingly interested in the world of quality whiskey: the flavors, the history, the regional varieties, and the culture was compelling enough that he had actually cut back on pool playing a bit. But he was still running tournaments and playing on a variety of teams and had recently won a doubles tournament with his friend Darian that would send him to his first Vegas APA tournament later that year.

Ross Schaefer and Gregg Taylor had their customary office set up on a table by the front door. The patio out back was once again a de facto satellite office to accommodate Taylor's heavy smoking, and as he went about his administrative duties, he alternated between analysis, old pool stores, and obnoxious commentary on passing servers and the state of the world. "Do you want to hear why transwomen are such good swimmers?" he asked. "No," I said, "I do not."[1]

Wake and Break had made it back to citywides, and Vatanagul told me they'd spent some time individually and collectively reflecting on getting knocked out of the World Pool Championships much earlier than they'd wanted to and, if they were being honest, much earlier than they thought they would. Vatanagul questioned his guidance as a captain while players fretted over the mistakes they'd made, but they concluded that there was no good reason for their substandard performance. They simply hadn't played as well as they should have from the beginning and couldn't find a toehold to bring them out of their funk.

"I was kind of done when we got knocked out," Damo Moloney said. "I couldn't wait to come home. But we were there a few days more."

The team made a strong return in the following session, however, and brought on some new people, including a quiet shooter named Isaac. The members were impressed by his bar-shooting skills, but nobody really knew him, and a few dicey interactions made them question the wisdom of introducing an unknown element into the chemistry of their tight-knit team.

Nearby was a team I hadn't seen in a while. For the first time in a long time Chalkie's Children had made it to citywides. Despite their making it this far, it seemed as though they had the same problem with player dedication that they'd had when I was on the team.

"Where's Kevin?" Chalkie asked.

"Dogwatching," someone answered.

"Dogwatching," Chalkie said, shaking his head. "Wow."

The team was eliminated not long after. Chalkie preferred to just get it over with.

"Citywides—that's like the whole weekend," he said.

Eventually, Wake and Break found themselves facing off against the Island of Lost Souls, a rematch with the team they'd beaten the year before. "This is payback," James Terronez told me, but Sonia Aujla seemed confused. "I don't even remember them—sorry," she said, unintentionally giving them a major diss.

---

1. Taylor requested that I include the following quote to summarize him as a character in this book and in life: "When you meet me, you either like me or you hate me, and it will take you five minutes to figure it out. I'll save you time: Sometimes it takes you twenty years to realize you don't like your best friend."

Aujla handily won the first match for Wake and Break, and the score was tipping in Wake and Break's favor when Terronez went up against Vatanagul. At one point, seeing my notebook, observers indicated that I should arbitrate a difficult shot, which I politely declined to do, citing the ethics of journalistic neutrality (not to mention I didn't want the teams' fate placed in my hands). Soon enough, however, Terronez's streak came to an end, and you could feel him getting frustrated when he couldn't fill any more pockets. Vatanagul seized the advantage, marking his pocket with his Deadpool figurine and taking the match.

"I psych myself out. That's the thorn in my side, especially on side pockets," Terronez said as he packed up his gear.

Content with the direction the evening had taken, Wake and Break could go home to rest, everyone excited to keep the rally going the next day.

"You play fourteen weeks and then it comes down to one game," Gregg Taylor said the following morning. "It's like Tom Brady going to the Super Bowl and there's a box in the middle of the field and they pull a golf ball out and you've gotta play with that."

I wasn't sure I followed, but the point was clear; the stakes were high.

Wake and Break kept their winning streak going, some matches harder fought than others, and they were ahead 5–3 when it was time for the new shooter, Isaac, to play. The match was in winning range, but the team was tense.

Isaac had taken a recent winning streak as confirmation of his talents to the degree that he'd been hostile to his teammates' advice, literally shrugging off an attempt at coaching. It was an audacious thing to do at such a juncture, and the rest of the team looked at each other worriedly. Isaac's opponent was also an entry-level 3, but one whose poise gave him an advantage; he was clearly more used to the APA format and the pressure of playing in a tournament. Moloney walked over to give Isaac some advice, and Isaac once again waved him off. Vatanagul and Aujla, looking in from the patio, felt their jaws drop. Isaac took a walloping game after game, but nobody bothered to try to give him any more advice, though I have to imagine he would have been more receptive as he got deeper in the hole.

Isaac was impassive as he burdened Wake and Break with a needless shutout, bringing the score to 5–6 in the opponent's favor. What had looked like a sure thing for Wake and Break was now dangerously inverted.

Schaefer poked his head out of the open glass door.

"Sudden Death," he told Vatanagul and Aujla.

It would be a race to one, a single winner-takes-all bout. Vatanagul would be the one to play. He pushed some negative thoughts to the back of his mind and played against his opponent Doug with such concentration that neither player looked up at the sudden explosion of noise from the street racers running high-speed circles around the block. Shrieking sirens and flashing police lights added to the chaos as "Free Bird" blared inside the pool hall. Everything came together in a whirling crescendo as the song's guitar solo reached its apex, and as the sirens and the song wound down, so did the action on the table. Vatanagul's opponent sank his final balls in an easy run, and Wake and Break's hopes to return to Las Vegas were ended.

The team huddled together for a quick debrief, grim expressions all around. Nobody seemed able to look in Isaac's direction. I started walking over but they were clearly not in a talking mood, let alone ready to concede that, hey, at least they'd had fun. It was a very unusual state for the team to be in given their normal high spirits, and the moment was all the more somber for it.

Kickin' Like Bruce likewise didn't bother with any justification for their underwhelming performance at the World Championships. The team simply hadn't played their best, and that was that. Brian Hale reckoned the team had another season or so after this one before the excitement and hope from their trip to Las Vegas wore off; after that, it would be back to normal, hoping for the best but not necessarily feeling that extra level of inspiration. Fortunately, they had no problem making it to citywides 2022, this time clad in new team shirts that had a cartoon Bruce Lee kicking a 9 ball.

In the semi-finals Kickin' Like Bruce was up against Garbage People, a 9-Ball team with Adina Fried and Eddie May. "We do a lot of [alcohol] shots when we play because . . . we're garbage people," Fried explained. The match-up couldn't have worked out better from the point of view of redemption, because it had been Kickin' Like Bruce that had knocked Garbage People out of the finals the previous year to secure the Vegas slot.

Fried held her own against the higher-ranked Bo Lee, but all day there had been whispering at each team's station. Some of the players on Garbage People felt that certain members of Kickin' Like Bruce had been playing slowly on purpose in order to run out the clock and push the match toward Sudden Death. To resolve the issue, the teams began assiduously using an hourglass to keep things moving.

Fried was bobbing along to the club bangers from the early 2000s playing loudly in the room. She held her stick out across the table and closed one eye to measure a shot.

"Take that!" she said, sinking a ball.

Her next shot was a scratch, and Lee picked up the ball.

"Take *that*!" he said.

But he missed, and he and his team groaned. Fried asked May to use his phone to play some songs by Machine Gun Kelly, one of her favorite artists at the moment, on the jukebox

"I can only play when I'm happy, and that makes me happy!" she said, sinking the 8 to take her match.

May was up next, and he had the dubious honor of playing what was arguably the most crucial game of Garbage People's run. Sudden Death had been declared, and Kickin' Like Bruce fielded Victor Mui for the game. May looked out at the table with heavy-lidded eyes: Mui was on his shitlist because it was this exact matchup last year that had cost his team the Vegas trip. Unfortunately, May felt in his bones that he was having an off night and tried to mentally reverse the curse.

"Shake it off, shake it off! You got this!" a teammate yelled from the sidelines.

Eventually, May's body went limp on the table after he not only missed but left the table wide open.

"FUCK!" he yelled as he stood back up.

Garbage People were out, which meant the 2022 citywide 9-Ball finals would be between Kickin' Like Bruce and Out, one of Jackson May's teams and so named because the members were always out playing pool.

The deciding match was under way at around 12:30 a.m. May was up first against Mui. May took the first game; Mui took the next two. Mui lined up his shot, but co-captain Wayne Wong came up to him and gently stopped him from shooting without a coach on what to do. The two conversed quietly and Mui returned to the table. The pressure was so intense that it appeared to eclipse itself and he transcended into a realm of preternatural calm. May knew he had to step up and wasn't afraid to do it. He crouched at the edge of the table as Mui took his shot, staring him in the eyes. Then, before the ball stopped moving, May jumped up to get ready to take his turn, as though Mui's shots weren't even worth paying attention to.

"I psyched him out, I got in his head," May said with a shrug.

Psych-outs or no, Mui eventually missed a shot that allowed May to sink everything he needed to, kicking Kickin' Like Bruce out of contention for Las Vegs in 2022. It appeared that the team had lost at citywides the same way they had lost in Vegas the year before: a long day of pool, a few points down, and the inability to cross the finish line at the crucial moment.

It had been a long night, a long session, and a long year, and it was time to head home.

CHAPTER 20

Duties of a Dynasty

Catching up with the Billiard Men and the BB Cues

The Billiard Men had been knocked out of the 2021 World Pool Championships by a team that Jackson May was convinced was sandbagging, leaving the team disheartened and leading him to delay his flight home twice so he could stay in Vegas to party away the loss. Five thousand dollars in the hole later, he decided it was time to head home. "I still haven't financially recovered from that trip," he said one evening at Surge Billiards.

The way the league handled the cheating and disqualification made team captain Eli Mancha more upset than he's felt in years, possibly the most consistently upset he's felt about something in his entire life.

"We're still bitter about it," he said. "We think about it every week."

"What was that team's name again that beat us?" a teammate asked.

"The Fuckin' Dickfaces?" Pierre Kasiansky offered.

The lingering feeling wasn't bitterness about losing; that was bad, of course, but losing is just part of the game. Given the amount of time (and money) Mancha had spent in the league, it was simply disappointing to feel wronged by something otherwise so personal. He'd briefly considered heading over to another pool organization, but that would mean leaving behind the friends and teammates he'd been playing with in the APA for years. For that reason he vowed to get over his disappointment and stay in the league.

"Hey! The coach is over!" Christine Arce said when the opponent's captain kept going up to talk to the shooter.

The man looked confused and explained that he was the coach.

"Yeah, I know! So you should know when to walk away from the table! The coach is over!"

Someone suggested that maybe the guy was new to the league and didn't know the etiquette.

No, Arce said firmly, that's not the case: He was a seasoned player who was trying to pull one over them.

"Christine . . . is a stickler for the rules," Mancha laughed. Though they were not afraid to speak up before, their experience at the World Pool Championships drove the team to become much more assertive.

The Billiard Men underwent significant handicap-related reshuffling after the trip to Las Vegas. Mancha said some of his best players did him a favor by leaving voluntarily instead of forcing him to make the call about who could stay and who had to go. "I miss Ricky," Arce sighed as we discussed this, as her boyfriend Ricky Torres had gone with the team to Vegas but had since been cut. "We both work a lot, and the team was a way for us to spend time together." The team was rebuilding, essentially from the ground up, to make up for these absences. At least three of the new players had never played an APA league match before.

Mike Desnoyers, one of the new Billiard Men, observed the evening's proceedings like a new kid in school. Desnoyers was a health insurance salesman originally from Vermont who'd moved to Chicago a few years earlier. He started going to Bang! Salon and learned of Mancha's obsession with pool; now he "wanted to be part of some of those pool stories." He was a good bar shooter but found that the routine of league play is a different beast altogether. When his food came, he ate almost self-consciously as teammates bantered around him. It was a hesitation I recognized—it was hard to put all the pieces together when you don't know the larger context, and he'd already received a bewildering amount of advice that had started on the drive over to the pool hall.

Mancha and Arce analyzed his game and chuckled at the rookie nature of his demeanor, such as when he tripped around the table or accidentally stood in his opponent's line of sight. Desnoyers turned around to ask Mancha a question, almost impaling him with his cue in the process. "Nice defense, Eli!" someone yelled as he artfully dodged the spear. Everyone laughed as Desnoyers reddened. Mancha corrected the error by gently lowering the cue and answered him.

All gaffs aside, Desnoyers was able to deliver on his shots, sinking a few balls in a row or knowing when to play defense. He started as a 3 but held his own against a seasoned 5, not a bad debut. "He's smart, competitive, into math, which uses the same side of the brain as pool," Mancha said. "He's gonna get good real fast." He unbuckled his Apple Watch and put it on the table next to his phone. "No distractions," he explained before going in for the slaughter, not letting his opponent win a single game.

Mancha had been busy as hell with Bang! Salon over the past few months as Chicagoans took halting steps toward a post-pandemic life. People were ready to emerge from the chrysalis of lockdown, to see and be seen again, and that necessitated a nice new haircut. His professional duties hadn't cut into his pool playing at all; he was playing just as often as he always had, and was on four separate teams.

"Sometimes it feels like I own a business to take away the stress of playing pool," he said a few weeks later. Unfortunately, the Billiard Men had since been knocked out of the Arlington Lanes Citywides and thus wouldn't be returning to Vegas in 2022, the result of a "bunch of stupid things" he didn't want to get into. He half-smiled as he shrugged, the gesture of someone who feels worse than he's letting on.

The question of Vegas 2022 answered, Mancha leaned fully into getting the new players into shape. They'd also recently taken on Linda, who'd been recruited from the ranks of Mancha's salon clients and who recently was on a bowling league, and Jan, whom Desnoyers knew from working out.

"Well, I wouldn't say 'dynasty,'" Kasiansky said. "But we are trying to get back to where we were."

By this point Desnoyers was helping the newbies acclimate to league play, and he'd grown noticeably more confident since I'd seen him last, cracking jokes and ribbing people when they ribbed him. Despite the first win, he experienced a ten-game losing streak before managing to flip it around and win ten of his next fourteen games, and he'd started the present session with a 4–0 lead. He downplayed my reading of what I thought were his nerves during his first match, saying he'd played a lot of sports in his life and was on the dance team in college, and so was used to performing in front of people.

"Here, you break it in," Desnoyers said, handing Jan a new stick, as it was time for Jan's debut match. "I got it for $30. It retails for $160."

He pulled out a yellow pool glove.

"You're gonna need one of these, too."

Having won his first game, Jan walked away from the table toward his jacket and pool bag. A teammate caught his arm and told him he wasn't through.

"You mean I get to play again?"

Mancha raised his eyebrows but then smiled and clapped him on the back.

"Yes," he said. "You get to play again."

Adina Fried's stature in the league had grown following the BB Cue's victory in Las Vegas. "People run around yelling 'I beat Adina,'" she said. "As a competitive person, this makes me mad." But as impressive and inspiring as the win had been, things had not been easy following the national championship.

The team went out for a hibachi dinner to celebrate its win (the tab ran to more than $1,000 and Fried picked it up, she said), and from her perspective, Vivian Ramos, who was not selected to play in the championship match, didn't seem to make much effort to talk to anyone. Three weeks later Fried's fiancé Eddie May threw the team a victory party, which Ramos attended, but she and Fried didn't even talk. It seemed the last conversation they'd ever have was the one about Ramos not playing in the finals.

The challenges of being a captain and league operator are things Fried regularly talks about with her therapist. But being able to make that difficult decision, and win because of it, was one of her proudest moments, and she'd been able to parlay the energy from the win into successes in other aspects of her life, such as demanding and receiving a substantial raise at work after finding out some of her subordinates were earning more than she was.

"It really took a lot for me to say no to her, that I was going to be the one who played," Fried said. "But if I'm going to respect myself for the rest of my life, it had to be me."

Teresa Jimmerson had moved away and needed to be replaced, and Christine Degrange, the shooter who played the final, tournament-winning match in Vegas, was no longer on the team either, following some mildly unpleasant confusion about work schedules. Fried's first in-person interaction with Degrange since the tournament—an awkward hello and quick parting of ways—occurred at the 2022 Women's League Citywides at Surge Billiards in Logan Square a few minutes before Fried laid all this out and brought me up to speed.

Joining the BB Cues was Taylor Peterson, an old friend of May's who'd been playing in the APA for four years but who was joining the BB Cues for the first time. "I just got a new cue, and I would love to buy a goddamn table one day," Peterson says, noting that she was going to be married in October and would be having pool tables at the reception.[1]

The 2022 women's citywides required a mini-playoff to determine the fourth of the final four teams. The team in the group with the lowest number of points that season, the Kick Shots, would be playing the league's newest team, the Cue Tease, for the fourth spot. The scrappy Kick Shots had the underdog status in their fight against the Cue Tease, who hadn't quite earned popular support for their Vegas ambitions because members were not known for being as gracious as others in the league and generally had what some saw as a haughty attitude they hadn't yet earned. The shooters had the skill to

---

1. They did end up having a table at the reception, but reportedly nobody played on it—guests were either non-players or too drunk to pay it much attention.

back up this posture, but the perceived lack of grace had compounded, and at this point their attitude made them seem almost like the bad guy team in a kids' sports movie.

"I like a good pool game, I always have," said Ross Schaefer from the sidelines. "People want to see passion. This is it."

The match between the Cue Tease and the Kick Shots was close and heated, and when I came back from briefly going across the street to get something to eat, everyone in the hall had gathered around the table, like a gang with spears circling around a fight. Kick Shots captain Allyson Nolde said the Cue Tease had no problem getting in their opponents' heads, interrupting them when they were shooting or not responding to questions about game play or rules. That kind of behavior was frustrating, she said, but "I gave it right back to them. They didn't know [that] when I get hacked off, I play better. Like, I can do this all day."

Eventually, the Kick Shots knocked the Cue Tease out of contention, and there was little in the way of farewell or congratulations; the Cue Tease packed their bags and walked out of Surge Billiards almost in unison. The Kick Shots were in the finals against the BB Cues, and the Kick Shots' surprising momentum almost made the BB Cues seem like the old guard ready to be retired by hungry newcomers.

But the BB Cues proved they were not to be trifled with. Alison Lewis won the final match, which sent the BB Cues to the World Pool Championships for the second year in a row. Everyone in the room burst into cheers and hugs no matter what team they were on or were rooting for. If the Kick Shots or the Velvet Tacos or another Chicago APA women's league team weren't the ones to make it, then they were thrilled to have the defending champs representing them once again on the national level.

Schaefer gathered the BB Cues near a table to sign the appropriate forms. "Wait a second . . ." he said, frowning at the score sheet. "Just kidding!" he said. This was met with laughs and groans, and the paperwork officially sending them to Las Vegas was signed. Moments later, the BB Cues were smiling for their year-end photos. They looked down the table confidently toward the camera—and toward another national title.

The Noble Game of (Local) Billiards

The Resonance of a Big Fish Story

> Physicians and surgeons of the highest rank among
> all nations have prescribed Billiards as the most
> exhilarating and the most beautiful of all games.
> Chess is too sedentary; and, besides, it turns out to be
> too irritating. To be well played, it taxes the intensest
> powers. Billiards can be played as a relaxation; It
> becomes an intense and exciting game only when
> the mind throws all its energies in that direction,
> and then it is full, often, of the spirit of heroism.
> —Isaac D. Guyer, *History of Chicago: Its Commercial
> and Manufacturing Interests and Industry*

One evening, when things were slow at City Pool Hall before league play kicked off for the night, bartender Krystal Glenn and barback Christian were talking about the time two-time World Champion Mika "The Iceman" Immonen showed up. Immonen is a professional pool player from Finland who often makes the rounds in the United States. He has friends and connections in Chicago and is known to pass through the city between tournament stops.

Pros often give clinics, lessons, and demo matches in their downtime, and they sometimes like to show up at a hall to test out the local competition. Christian the bartender recalled players "lined up like fanboys" for a chance to play against the respected Immonen the last time he passed through.

"And you know what?" Christian said. "I beat him."

An otherwise quiet guy sitting at the bar perked up.

"No, you didn't," he said.

"Yes, I did!" Christian said. "He scratched on the nine. I beat him on a technicality."

"Well, congratulations then," the man said, still squinting at him skeptically.

Christian's boast was basically the pool equivalent of a big fish story, and it wasn't uncommon for claims about winning shots or unexpected victories to be challenged or one-upped. For obvious reasons, the idea of a local player beating someone like Mika Immonen should be immediately challenged, though it's possible it could have happened as Christian said. As my time in the APA proved, there were more than a few players good enough to hold their own against high-level players. But if the average local player *did* beat a professional, that was something everyone could be proud of because it spoke for the toughness and skill of the Chicago scene.

There was a similar kind of collective pride as the BB Cues made their way to the APA women's league championships two years in a row. These were certainly tough ladies who everyone knew had earned the right to defend their title and Chicago's reputation in 2022.

Unfortunately, an unprecedented back-to-back national title was not meant to be. The BB Cues went down in the fourth round, vanquished by a team from New Orleans who let loose such an intense roar when the

The BB Cues returned to Las Vegas as defending women's champs. New teammate Trisha Kimber prepares to shoot as the rest of the team looks on. (Photo courtesy of the author.)

final ball was sunk that it bordered on the frightening. While Chicago pool players didn't feel the vicarious thrill of another championship, the BB Cues were welcomed warmly when they were back on their home turf. They had a lot to show for their two or more years of serious grinding, and in the next session the team felt content to relax a little, to lean into the atmosphere of the game and appreciate the simple joy of being part of the community.

It's always great to see where the game takes people, the APA's Jason Bowman said, both on the table and off. There's the thrill of competition and the personal satisfaction of watching your game improve, but players have also found love, found friends, deepened bonds and professional networks, encouraged recovery, and comforted each other during times of loss. Bowman himself met his wife in the offices of the APA, the direct result of the game of pool.

"People ask, 'How have you worked there for twenty-something years?' It's because I have no qualms about selling what I sell. I don't want to sell life insurance, I don't want to sell funerals to people," he said. "I get to sell something that helps people, that makes people feel good about themselves, brings people together. . . . I want to feel good about what I do, and maybe one day my kids will work at the company and be proud of what they do."

Over the course of working on this book, I met plenty of pool players who plan their vacations around visits to pool halls, have pool tables at their weddings, develop teaching tools, brag about beating professionals, and consider buying a home *only* if there is enough space for a table. Although it's a huge honor to compete in Las Vegas (and a great party when you do), it was also clear that winning such a trip is ultimately beside the point.

"It's pretty simple," said Adina Fried, florist, pool player, and captain of a national championship team. "We identify as pool players. That's the first thing we tell people. That's just who we are."

Acknowledgments

A few months after attending the 2022 APA World Pool Championships that close out this book, I was wandering around Tirana, Albania, on vacation with my sweetheart when I saw a knee-level illuminated sign that said "Bilardo" above a stairwell that led to an open doorway. The familiar sound of clacking balls filled the air, and the door opened to a long, narrow room with three eight-foot tables set longways end to end, the back table open to play and already set with balls in a triangle. The owner, Erwin, took a break from teaching a young couple how to shoot and welcomed us in, informing us that each game cost one hundred leke, or approximately $1. Two guys were playing on the table next to us, and we commenced shooting next to them in a room outfitted with wooden paneling, seats that were legless plastic chairs affixed to a bench, and miscellaneous items like bikes and scooters piled up for sale. Erwin continued to help the budding players adopt the correct stance, but he also kept an eye out for whenever someone sank the 8 ball and ended the game, and he'd come over to insert a metal token into the table to release the balls for the next round.

Despite my complete inability to speak Albanian, the scene was familiar and universal. Eventually, my gal and I were the only ones left, and we chatted with Erwin as best we could about the game and the preferred way to play in our respective countries. I had my phone with me and showed him pictures of the Las Vegas tournament. He nodded appreciatively at the rows and rows of tables surrounded by players. "Wow," Erwin said. "Women league—very good." He said he'd been to Greece, Germany, Switzerland, Bulgaria, and a few other countries to compete, and he almost always competed in 8-Ball; he strongly disliked 9-Ball, he noted, because it was too quick and not strategic enough. He said the most popular pool game in Albania is "61," in which the lowest-numbered ball on the table must be struck first before hitting the object ball. (The game is insanely hard, Eddie May said—imagine always having to do only combo shots.)

We would see and hear bilardo halls throughout the rest of our trip, and while we didn't go any deeper into Albanian pool culture than shooting a few games here and there, it was clear that, as in Chicago, there was an obvious love for the game among its local adherents. If we wanted to do, we no doubt could have sought out whatever kind of game we wanted—a friendly round with Erwin, a slightly more serious match against any of the guys in tracksuits nearby, or even higher-stakes games in even more obscure little halls.

Although I'm still a terrible pool player (and perhaps more frustrated than ever because I know what I *should* do but just can't physically do it), I was very appreciative of the time and generosity of the people in Chicago who let me hang around and helped me understand the game better than I otherwise would have been able to. The door had been opened to many interesting, enjoyable, funny, and startling experiences, whether in Chicago, Albania, or the pool halls of Texas, where I currently live. And while one of the difficulties of being a writer is that you spend a ton of time in the world you're writing about but then may not ever return to it once your research is over, thanks to my work on this project I have such a great group of people to catch up with whenever I'm in Chicago.

On that note, I extend my deepest thanks to hall employees, tournament organizers, inventors, and pool fanatics of every stripe (and solid), everyone who invited me to tag along, shared their perspective, and allowed me to get really invasive about why they're drawn to the game. Thanks in particular to Eddie May, Adina Fried, Eli Mancha, Jutichai Vatanagul, Brian Hale, Gregg Taylor, and Reggie Julun for being especially helpful guides—it really means a lot that you were interested in this project and that we were able to spend the time together as a result. This book would not have been the same, or even possible, without the immense help of Ross Schaefer, who brought me into the league, showed me how it worked, and set me up with the first interviews that turned me loose in the larger world of pool. And I deeply appreciate the patience, insight, and humor of everyone I talked to on teams, in the league, in the halls, in Vegas, or anywhere we might have connected. This was a fun, fun project to work on in every way, and I hope this book does justice to the stories and thrills as you lived them.

Thank you to Martha Bayne at the University of Illinois Press for championing this book and for her insight and hustle, Jane Zanichkowsky for the excruciatingly precise and immensely helpful copyedits, and everyone else at the press for their work on this book. Much gratitude to family and friends who were kind enough to smile and nod when I talked once again about the nuances of pool and its history, to my good friend Alison Rieger for the index that will no doubt be helpful to future scholars, and a special shout-out to the well-worn table in the mezzanine of my former workplace for giving me a respite from writing about the renewable energy industry and sparking the idea that amateur pool might be an interesting world to explore. Going back even further, cheers to my Aunt Leann and Uncle Steve for having a really nice table when I was a kid and letting me roll balls madly across it like spaceships in battle; though they probably looked on in dismay, I can credit that table with showing me there is something inherently great about the game, even when I realized there was more to it than rolling balls around chaotically.

My mom and dad not only bought me a pool cue when I was a freshman in college to shoot around on my dorm's table before I made friends but have also endlessly encouraged my brother and me to follow wherever our curiosity and interests take us. There is so much I admire about you both and the lives you've led, and you both certainly warrant biographies of your own. And finally, infinite adoration and gratitude to my dear Pamela, the most perceptive, thoughtful, hilarious, and *seria* ray of light and companion I could ever know—our dreams go together like solids and stripes, a beautiful shared ballet across the green felt of life.

Bibliography

A Chicago pool fanatic named David Bond was putting together a website called the Chicago Billiard Museum to serve as the clearinghouse for everything history and pool in Chicago. The website was full of timelines, newspaper clippings, advertisements, tournament coverage, and scans of pool books long since forgotten. Unfortunately, Bond died in 2018, and it appears any further work on the project has stalled. Although the website Chicagobilliardmuseum.org has been taken down, a wealth of articles and files is still accessible through the Wayback Machine at https://webcf.waybackmachine.org/.

It would have been interesting to see how this online museum project developed, and I want to extend my gratitude to the late founder for the significant effort he made to compile all this material. His work was a huge help in writing this book and is a tremendous resource for pool fans, historians, and scholars in Chicago and beyond.

Books and Scholarship

Bentivegna, Freddy "The Beard." *The "Encyclopedia" of Pool Hustlers*. Freddythebeard, Inc., 2013.

Chang, Sheng-chieh, and George S. Baus. "Precarious Distraction and Carious Extraction: Nitrous Oxide During the 'Second World Billiards Tournament.'" *Journal of Anesthesia History*, vol. 3, no. 4 (September 2017).

Chicago's First Half-Century. Inter-Ocean, 1883.

Cohen, Kenneth. "Billiards and American Culture, 1660–1860." MA thesis, University of Delaware, 2002.

Cramer, John D. "Health Factories and Palaces of Pleasure: Bowling, Billiards, and the Chicago 'Rec,' 1895–1929." MS thesis, School of the Art Institute of Chicago, 2011.

Fensch, Thomas. *The Lions and the Lambs*. New Century, 1970.

Gems, Gerald. "The German Turners and the Taming of Radicalism in Chicago." *International Journal of the History of Sport*, vol. 26, no. 13 (October 2009).

Gems, Gerald. *Windy City Wars*. Scarecrow, 1997.

Gorn, Elliot, ed. *Sports in Chicago*. University of Illinois Press in cooperation with the Chicago History Museum, 2008.

Helfert, Jay. *Pool Wars: On the Road to Hell and Back with the World's Greatest Money Players.* iUniverse, 2012.

Hoppe, Willie, and Thomas Emmett Crozier, eds. *Thirty Years of Billiards.* G. P. Putnam's Sons, 1925.

Kogan, Rick. *Brunswick: The Story of an American Company from 1845 to 1985.* Brunswick Corporation, 1985.

Laurence, Ewa Mataya, and Thomas C. Shaw. *The Complete Idiot's Guide to Pool & Billiards.* Alpha, 1999.

McKenna, Brian. "Sputtering Towards Respectability: Chicago's Journey to the Big Leagues." Society for American Baseball Research, 2015. https://sabr.org/journal/article/sputtering -towards-respectability-chicagos-journey-to-the-big-leagues/.

Melendy, Royal L. "The Saloon in Chicago, Il.," *American Journal of Sociology,* vol. 6 (January 1901).

The Pioneer Arcade Landmark Designation Report. City of Chicago, December 8, 2022.

Polsky, Ned. *Hustlers, Beats, and Others.* 2d ed. Lyons, 1985.

Riess, Steven A., ed. *A Companion to American Sport History.* Wiley Blackwell, 2014.

San Juan, Eric. *The Films of Martin Scorsese.* Rowman & Littlefield, 2020.

Reportage

Associated Press. "Highly Decorated Vet Who Killed 400 Nazis." *Chicago Tribune,* September 19, 1988.

Baird, Sarah. "Life and Death of the American Pool Hall." *Punch,* January 23, 2015. https:// punchdrink.com/articles/the-life-and-death-of-the-american-pool-hall/.

Ballew, Jonathan. "Meet the Apocalypsticks, The 8-Ball Queens of Cary's Lounge— And World Pool Champions." blockclubchicago.org, September 3, 2019. https:// blockclubchicago.org/2019/09/03/meet-the-apocalypsticks-the-8-ball-queens-of-carys -lounge-and-national-pool-champions.

Bowman, Jason. "Chicago's Apocalypsticks Won the 2019 APA Ladies 8-Ball Championship." *Beechwood Reporter,* September 3, 2019.

Booth, Steve. "Rack 'em up with Freddy 'The Beard' Bentivegna, part 1." onepocket.org, 2005. http://www.onepocket.org/BentivegnaInterview1.htm.

Booth, Steve. "Rack 'em up with Freddy 'The Beard' Bentivegna, part 2." onepocket.org, 2005. http://www.onepocket.org/BentivegnaInterview2.htm.

Boyle, Robert H. "The Bizarre History of American Sport." *Sports Illustrated,* January 8, 1962.

"A Brief History of Billiards: A Pictorial Chronology and Timeline of the Continuing Evolution of Pool." *The Hyper Texts,* n.d. thehypertexts.com/History%20of%20Billiards%20Pool%20 Chronology.htm.

Butler, Patrick. "'Pied Piper of Pool' Van Eck Brings Billiards to Local Boys and Girls Clubs." *Chicago Gazette,* February 4, 2017.

Cepeda, Esther J. "Confessions of a Pool-Hall Junkie: For Those with the Stroke, It's a Snap to Separate the 'Eggs' from the 'Sharks.'" *Chicago Sun-Times,* October 7, 2007.

"City Pool Hall." chibarproject.com. https://chibarproject.com/reviews/citypoolhall/.

"A Complete Guide Enabling Visitors to More Readily See and Appreciate the Great Inter-State Exposition of Chicago." Inter-State Exposition of Chicago, 1873.

Cramer, John D. "'A Recreational Masterpiece' on Chicago's Milwaukee Avenue." Personal blog, February 4, 2013. https://johndcramer.wordpress.com/2013/02/04/congress-arcade-chicag/.

"Cruel Summer." *Billiards Digest,* November 2007.

Daday, Eileen O. "Arlington Heights Man Passes Love of Pool to Kids." *Daily Herald* (Chicago), September 7, 2016.

Dreher, Christopher. "What Kevin Trudeau Doesn't Want You to Know." *Salon*, July 2005.

"8-Ball Legends to Compete in World Championship Match." International Pool Tour press release, July 21, 2005.

Eisenberg, John. "Off to the Races." *Smithsonian*, August 2004.

Fredman, Alan. "Chalk One Up for Pool as a Growing Sport." *St. Louis Post-Dispatch*, November 19, 1985.

Gorn, Elliot. "Creation of Chicago Sports." *Encyclopedia of Chicago*, http://www.encyclopedia.chicagohistory.org/pages/1184.html.

Graff, Keir. "Mis-Cue." Newcity Chicago, July 25, 1999. newcitychicago.com/home/daily/feature/pool070599.html.

Guyer, Isaac D. *History of Chicago: Its Commercial and Manufacturing Interests and Industry.* Church, Goodman, and Cushing, 1862. https://archive.org/details/historyofchicago00guye/page/n7/mode/2up.

Hoover, Gary. "Billiards, Bowling, and Boating: 175 Years of Brunswick." americanbusinesshistory.org, October 16, 2020. https://americanbusinesshistory.org/billiards-bowling-and-boating-175-years-of-brunswick/.

Jackson, David, and Gary Marx. "Chicago Fugitive Arrested After *Tribune* Investigation." *Chicago Tribune*, February 28, 2012.

Joravsky, Ben. "Hustled by Freddy 'the Beard' Bentivegna." *Chicago Reader*, April 30, 2014.

Kantowski, Ron. "Pool Players Converge for World's Largest Tournament at Westgate." *Las Vegas Review-Journal*, August 16, 2017.

Kim, Jae-Ha. "Champs, Novices Queue Up at Pool Hall." *Chicago Sun-Times*, September 11, 1994.

King, Mason. "In the Black." *Billiards Digest*, April 2008.

Krause, Kitry. "The Boys at the Billiard Cafe." *Chicago Reader*, May 12, 1988.

Leavitt, Aimee. "RIP Freddy 'the Beard' Bentivegna." chicagoreader.com, June 20, 2014. https://chicagoreader.com/blogs/rip-freddy-the-beard-bentivegna/.

Leavitt, Aimee. "The Twilight of Freddy the Beard." *Chicago Reader*, April 2014. https://chicagoreader.com/arts-culture/the-twilight-of-freddy-the-beard/.

Logan, Bob. "Sharpening Their Game Keeps Seniors from Getting Behind 8-Ball." *Chicago Tribune*, June 2, 1988.

Maclean, Norman F. "Billiards Is a Good Game." *University of Chicago Magazine*, Summer 1975.

Mandernach, Mark. "The First Family of Billiards." *Chicago Tribune*, February 6, 1994.

Mather, Victor. "After Much Effort, an 'Unbreakable' Record in Straight Pool Is Topped." *New York Times*, May 28, 2019.

McGraw, Eliza. "Ruth McGinnis: Queen of Billiards." smithsonianmag.com, March 22, 2018. https://www.smithsonianmag.com/history/ruth-mcginnis-queen-billiards-180968563/.

Mills, Marja. "Teen Pool Hall Hits Spot in Crystal Lake." *Chicago Tribune*, October 17, 1989.

"The New Brunswick and Balke Billiard Factory: A Triumph in German Diligence and Enterprise." *Der Western*, December 12, 1875.

"No Hustlers but Sharks Galore." *Chicago Tribune*, October 31, 2002.

"Paul Newman Adrift in the Cold." *Chicago Sun-Times*, March 21, 1986.

Pratt, Gregory. "Old-School Pool Hall's End of an Era a Reminder to Cherish Special Places." *Chicago Tribune*, March 30, 2017.

Revsine, Barbara. "A New Look for the Old Pool Hall: Rack Up Another One for Yuppies." *Chicago Tribune*, October 20, 1989.

Rose, Don. "How We Got Dr. King to Shoot Pool to Make Him More of a Chicago 'Street Guy.'" *Chicago Sun-Times*, April 16, 2018.

Sampey, Patrick. "iCue—Thomas Van Eck." *Inside Pool*, May 11, 2020. https://insidepoolmag.com /icue-thomas-van-eck/.

Selvan, Ashok. "After 48 Years, Pool Hall to Serve More Than Pizza Puffs." *Chicago Reader*, November 9, 2017.

Selzer, Adam. "The Scariest Gangster You've Never Heard Of." *Time Out Chicago*, March 3, 2015. https://www.timeout.com/chicago/blog/the-scariest-chicago-gangster-youve -never-heard-of-031315.

Selzer, Adam. "The Strange Tale of the Cardinella Gang." mysteriouschicago.com, August 6, 2014. https://mysteriouschicago.com/the-strange-tale-of-the-cardinella-gang/.

Span, Alison. "Cold Case: Police Looking into Murder of 'Biloxi Mike' with Fresh Set of Eyes." Wlox.com, December 6, 2019. wlox.com/2019/12/06/cold-case-police-looking -into-murder-biloxi-mike-with-fresh-set-eyes/.

Struett, David. "7 Relatives Hospitalized After Drunken Fight at Jefferson Park Billiards Hall: Police." *Chicago Sun-Times*, August 4, 2020.

"Trudeau to Anxious Players: Trust Me, the Money's Coming." *Billiards Digest*, October 20, 2006. http://www.billiardsdigest.com/new_news/display_article?id=722.

Tucker, Ernest. "Cool Pool Halls Dress Up Image of Popular Game." *Chicago Sun-Times*, October 27, 1989.

Vitello, Barbara. "Home of the Great Ones: The Best Players Show Up on Cue at Chris's Billiards." *Daily Herald* (Chicago), June 28, 2002.

Ward, Joe. "Edgewater's Pressure Billiards Pool Hall Closing After This Weekend: 'We Thank Everyone for Their Support.'" Block Club Chicago, February 10, 2022. https:// blockclubchicago.org/2022/02/10/edgewaters-pressure-billiards-pool-hall-closing-after-this -weekend-we-thank-everyone-for-their-support/.

"We're the American Poolplayers Association." *St. Louis Post-Dispatch*, July 17, 1994.

Williams, Pete. "IPT Pool Tour Goes off with a Bang." buzzle.com, December 11, 2005. https:// www.buzzle.com/editorials/12–11–2005–83690.asp.

Weich, Susan. "Pool Players Can Take a Cue from These Two." *St. Louis Post-Dispatch*, January 12, 2011.

Wertheim, L. Jon. "Jump the Shark." *New York Times*, November 24, 2007.

Websites of Various Pool Organizations and Vendors

American Poolplayers Association: poolplayers.com

AZ Billiards Forum: azbilliards.com

Billiard Congress of America: bca-pool.com

Chicagology: chicagology.com (especially the sections about Tom Foley and Brunswick)

Colorado State's Billiard Club: https://billiards.colostate.edu/

Imperial: https://www.imperialusa.com/.

Pool Dawg: pooldawg.com

Pool History: poolhistory.com

Scott Lee's Traveling College of Billiard Knowledge: poolknowledge.com

Index

International Olympic Committee, 84
International Pool Tour (IPT), 83–84
internet as a learning tool, 53, 65, 82, 93, 102
IPT North American Open, 83
Isasi, Valentin, 55
Island of Lost Souls, 11, 55, 144

Japanese players, 21, 90, 104, 111
Japanese Poolplayers Association, 21n4
Jenkins, Richard, Jr., 123
Jet Johnson, 32
Jimmerson, Teresa, 47, 132, 151
JR's Queen Bees, 117
Julun, Reggie "The Riddler": administrative duties, *89*, 89–90, 91–92, 143; profession, 88, 95–96, 143; team play, 15–16, 88–89, 95, 143; World Pool Championships, 121
Just Make It, 118

Kasiansky, Pierre, 128, 148, 150
Kerryman, The, 51
Kickin' Like Bruce: citywide tournaments, 146–47; membership, *27–28*; 9-ball, 27; team apparel, 146; World Championships, 28, 101, 127, 129–30, 146
Kick Push, 54
Kick Shots, 151–52
King, Martin Luther, Jr., 91
King Louis XIV, 29
Knights Templar, 29
Kohler, Florian "Venom," 113

Ladies (a.k.a. LFG), 117
Las Vegas: gambling, 60, 148; World Pool Championship, 2, 60, 104–5, 109–10
Laurance, Ewa, 42n, 50, 133–37
Lebron, Mike, 126n
Lee, Jeanette "The Black Widow," 50, 82
Lee, Vincent "Bo," 27–28, 129, 146–47
legality, 25, 29
Lewis, Alison: BB Cues, 47, 102, 152; World Pool Championships, 47, 116, 131, 134–35
Lincoln, Abraham, 29

lingo: going rackless, 14; lag, 13; sandbagging, 23; squirt, 44
Luck Runs Out, 116

Magic City Shooters, 117
Malkani, Cathy, 93
Mancha, Eli: The Billiard Men, 12, 98–100, 102; equipment, 43; initiating sandbagging investigation, 128–29, 148; Mancha United, 38; profession, 38–39, 149–50; team captain, 38–39, 114, 118, 148–50; World Pool Championships, 38–39, 102, 114–15, 118, 123
Mancha United, 38
Manilow, Barry, 111
Marie's Golden Cue, 37, 69, 71, 74n
Mary, Queen of Scots, 29n2
Matchroom Sport, 81
May, Eddie: approach to pool, 63; betting and gambling, 60–61, 63–66; City Pool Hall, 46; Garbage People, 146–47; Hundreds over Hardware, 61; profession, 63; Scotch doubles tournament, 61; World Pool Championships, 111–14
May, Jackson: Billiard Men, 62, 97–99, 111; Out, 147; profession, 62; World Pool Championships, 111, 118, 129, 148
McDevitt, James, 70n2
McGinnis, Ruth, 49
merchandise, 104, 111–12, 119–22, *120*
Merchant, Wahib, 68–69, 72, 78
Metal Billiards, 36
Mexican Johnny, 32
Midnight Strokers, 11, 14
Minassian, Ted, 69
Mingaud, François, 42
Minnesota Fats (Rudolf Walderone), 36, 36n4
misogyny in pool, 48–50
Moloney, Damo "Blackout," 3–4, 51–52, 55–56, 144, 145
Morales, Cesar. *See* Reyes, Efren
Morse, Ryan, 97
Mosconi, Willie, 81, 83n
Mosconi Cup, 81, 82
Mui, Jennifer, 130
Mui, Victor, 147

DYLAN TAYLOR-LEHMAN is a journalist and writer and the author of *Sealand: The True Story of the World's Most Stubborn Micronation and Its Eccentric Royal Family* and *Dance of the Trustees: On the Astonishing Concerns of a Small Ohio Township.*

The University of Illinois Press
is a founding member of the
Association of University Presses.

_____

Composed in 11.25/13 Adobe Garamond
with Gotham display
by Kirsten Dennison
at the University of Illinois Press
Manufactured by Versa Press, Inc.

University of Illinois Press
1325 South Oak Street
Champaign, IL 61820-6903
www.press.uillinois.edu